T5-BCI-323

TRANSACTIONS

of the

American Philosophical Society

Held at Philadelphia for Promoting Useful Knowledge

VOLUME 81, Part 7

ST. JOSEPH'S UNIVERSITY

3 9353 00273 3788

DC
34.5
.R8
H377
1991

Russian Refugees
In France and the United States
Between the World Wars

I know how men in exile feed on

dreams of hope

. . . Aeschylus

James E. Hassell

Copyright1991 © by The American Philosphical Society

Library of Congress Catalogue Card Number 91-76294
International Standard Book Number 0-87169-817-X
US ISSN 0065-9746

For my mother and father

Alexander Nevsky Cathedral, Paris.
Headquarters of the Russian Orthodox Church in exile.
Photograph by Edward J. Hassell.

CONTENTS

PREFACE

This study was undertaken before the advent of *glasnost* and *perestroika*. The astonishing transformations that have been occurring under the leadership of Mikhail Gorbachev now lend additional poignancy to the lives of the Russian exiles that are the subjects of this book. At long last a regeneration of their lost homeland, a liberation of the kind for which so many had hoped, seems to be under way. At the very least we can be sure that the era of Soviet history to which they belonged is now definitely closed. The Russian White refugees will always be encompassed in that chapter of Soviet history dominated by the sinister figure of Stalin. It was not for them to see the "New Russia" which we of the 1990s now witness.

I wish particularly to thank two institutions for allowing me the opportunity to immerse myself in this vanished world of the White refugees. The Philadelphia College of Textiles and Science granted me sabbatical leave, and the American Philosophical Society provided financial support. My investigations were significantly aided by the staffs of the Textile College Pastore Library, the Balch Institute for Ethnic Studies, the New York Public Library Slavonic Division, the Bakhmeteff Archive of Columbia University's Rare Book and Manuscript Library, the YWCA National Board Archives, the American National Red Cross Archives, the National Archives of the United States, and, in Paris, the Archives nationales and Bibliothèque nationale.

Anatole and Galina Forostenko first suggested to me the basic idea for this book. John Murray and Vera Yunus put me in touch with émigrés willing to recount their personal stories. Such individual reminiscences that people in both the United States and France graciously shared were an invaluable check on the written sources. Various stages of researching and writing were furthered with the aid of Rodney Carlisle, Lynn Harrison, John Long, and Charlie Richardson.

I thank my many colleagues at the Philadelphia College of Textiles and Science who read portions of the manuscript and offered their suggestions and encouragement. Dean William Andrews and my department chair, William Brown, deserve special acknowledgment for helping me to launch this enterprise. And two typists of remarkable patience and skill, Monica DeCarlo and Barbara Frank, carried the project through to its end. The person who has most helped me to understand what it means to leave one's homeland is Sigrid Weltge.

I. Introduction

Revolution in 1917 brutally shattered old Russia in all its aspects. Something on the order of a million and a half people consequently fled or were expelled from the territory of the former Russian Empire. The fate of those who landed on these shores is of particular interest to Americans, and I shall describe the experiences of Russians who arrived in the United States between the two world wars. But the spiritual center of the entire Russian diaspora was France, particularly Paris, so France must be part of the story. Many of the refugees who ultimately settled in the United States passed through France. Many had connections in France; therefore, some knowledge of the French situation is crucial for an understanding of the émigrés in this country and indeed throughout the world. Although France and the United States were more hospitable to the Russians than many countries, still the life of the refugee was hard. The efforts of émigrés to make that life in exile meaningful, their daily struggles for existence, are the raw material for this study.

Russians fleeing the 1917 revolution were part of a larger current that has disturbed this century. The twentieth century has been the age of the refugee, the person in flight from repression and, often, death. So far, European refugees alone have numbered about 45,000,000. The chaos of wars and revolutions and the gaps in records make these statistics of human upheaval only estimates. What of the great nineteenth-century European migration to the New World? Several million were victims of political or religious persecution, but the great majority set out willingly, anticipating a better life. The nineteenth century was a time of unprecedented voluntary emigration by Europeans. Some 60,000,000 of them left home. The Russians who concern us were victims of massive destructive forces peculiar to our own age.

Those who fled the revolution constituted a rich ethnic mix. They included, among others, Ukrainians, Poles, Balts, and Jews, as well as Russians proper. Immigration records seldom distinguished among these ethnic groups. My intent, however, is to concentrate on the story of those who considered themselves "Russian," who spoke the Russian language, and who for the most part adhered to the Orthodox Church.

The Russian refugees of the 1920s included a high proportion of middle and upper class people, many educated and professional. Their class and values set them apart from other waves of Russian émigrés in the twentieth century. Pre-World War I emigration out of Russia was largely by peasants, who set out for America dreaming of making their fortunes and then returning to settle in their native villages. Similarly, Russian dis-

1

placed persons after World War II were predominantly peasant and working class in origin.

Those Russians who became exiles in the 1920s were the last generation to share intellectual and cultural values with western Europeans. On those planes a commonality of outlook linked Russians with their western counterparts. But under Soviet tutelage this changed. New generations grew up in strict isolation from western European and American culture and thought patterns. Those intellectuals and professionals who have left the Soviet Union since the Second World War have felt themselves a group apart. The intellectual, even popular, climate of the West is alien to them, whereas it had not been for their predecessors of the 1920s.

One might then expect that the path was smoother for those in the 1920s who were entering a somewhat familiar world. France, especially, had a very powerful cultural attraction for the Russian upper classes. Young Frenchwomen for generations had found employment in Russia, teaching their language to the children of the aristocracy. The French Riviera since the middle of the nineteenth century had been a vacation spot favored by wealthy Russians, including the royal family itself. Unlike the pleasure seekers on the Riviera, there were colonies of Russian intellectuals in Paris, New York, and other western cities, usually living under onerous conditions. Almost all of them were socialists or liberals who opposed the tsarist government. Almost all of them welcomed the revolution. But the overthrow of the tsar in March 1917 was one thing; the Bolshevik seizure of power in November 1917 was another. Many who approved of revolution did not approve of the Bolsheviks. Garbled reports of events in Russia threw the Parisian and New York intellectuals into an uproar. And into that tempest were precipitated thousands of new exiles representing a wide spectrum of political views. Political passions rode very high throughout the 1920s and kept the émigré community in an agitated condition, divided against itself.

The paths the refugees traveled were extremely diverse. During the first five years after the Bolshevik seizure of power, 1918-1922, the greatest number of those who were to leave started out into the unknown. Most legendary is the large-scale evacuation from Crimean ports in November 1920. Bolshevik or "Red" forces were relentlessly pressing southward in the civil war, and the opposing "Whites" faced annihilation. The last of General Wrangel's White Army, accompanied by many civilians, made their way across the Black Sea. In the course of one week, 126 vessels carried more than 150,000 people from the Crimean ports to the Bosporus Straits. First stop was Constantinople or camps scattered from Gallipoli to the Dardenelles. Some remained in Constantinople for years. Others moved elsewhere in the Middle East or beyond.

White Russians eventually found their way into every European country. Many thousands were attracted to each of the Slavic states where they felt some bonds of kinship, and the newly founded government of

Czechoslovakia proved to be the most hospitable. Intellectuals and professional people were more liable to find employment in Czechoslovakia than elsewhere in Eastern Europe. A lively academic community developed in Prague around the university and Russian publishing houses. The Czech government provided higher education to 3,000 Russians.

The bulk of the emigration pushed into Western Europe. By 1920 560,000 Russians had settled in Germany, making it the first cultural center of the diaspora where the émigrés began to formulate their views about their fate, their relationships to "Russia" and the world of exile, and their problematic future. It was in Berlin that Vladimir Dmitrievich Nabokov, father of the famous novelist, was assassinated in 1922. He was a moderate constitutionalist and fell victim (a mistaken target) to two Russian émigré right-wing extremists.

In 1924 Paris replaced Berlin as the White center. Catastrophic inflation of the German mark and greater employment opportunities in France caused a massive shift. Most of the émigrés moved from Germany to France; many stayed in that country but others moved onward. Through a multitude of routes 20,000 Whites reached the United States and twice that number landed in Canada. About 15,000 settled in the British Isles. Opportunities were limited in South America, generally to arduous agricultural labor or military service, but 3,000 made their way, usually to Brazil, Argentina, or Paraguay.

There was also the Far Eastern exodus. A major stream of refugees pushed through Siberia where the Russian civil war persisted into 1923. They made up a quarter million people, most of them settling in China, especially in Manchuria. Relatively few moved on to Korea, Japan, Indochina, and the Philippines. Thousands eventually reached the West Coast of North America. Approximately 2,000 ended their odyssey in Australia.

Chinese treaty ports harbored thousands of White Russians who joined the European enclaves there. But the White émigrés were denied the extraterritorial privileges that other Europeans enjoyed, and some of them acquired Chinese citizenship. A vigorous Russian colony of 19,000 developed in the great port city of Shanghai where the Whites comprised two-thirds of the European inhabitants. This bustling, cosmopolitan metropolis sustained the Russians in positions ranging from doctors and lawyers to shop-owners, domestic servants, peddlers, and prostitutes. With their own churches, stores, restaurants, and newspapers, in short, a "little Russia," the Shanghai colony found a degree of solace in exile.

Harbin, central city of Manchuria, was the most congenial of all Far Eastern exile sites. It was essentially a "Russian" city, founded in 1898 by Russian builders of the Chinese Eastern Railway. (The Chinese government had granted Russia the right to construct this branch of the Trans-Siberian Railroad to Vladivostok.) About 85,000 White émigrés initially settled in Harbin and found themselves in a thoroughly Russian milieu. If

Paris was the cultural center of the world-wide diaspora, Harbin was certainly the cultural center of the Far Eastern contingent. It maintained Russian institutions of higher education which had counterparts outside the Soviet Union only in Paris and Prague. Russian theater and opera and literary life throve in Harbin. A large number of militant émigré organizations coexisted with a U.S.S.R. Consulate and numerous Soviet officials, thus promoting often fevered political polemics. But even after the Japanese occupation of 1932 Harbin was economically prosperous, and the émigrés there were generally better off than anywhere else in the Far East.[1]

A few Russians had been abroad at the time of the revolution, notably those on diplomatic missions, and simply never returned. The new Soviet regime itself expelled over 160 of the country's foremost intellectuals in the autumn of 1922.[2] They were shipped either to Stettin or to Constantinople, all accused of opposition to the new party in power. Prominent among their number were theologian Sergei Bulgakov, philosopher Nicolai Berdiaev, historian Alexander Kizevetter, and sociologist Pitirim Sorokin.

Although many refugees had enjoyed high status and positions in Russia, they very seldom achieved comparable standing in exile. Their most serious problem between the world war was poverty, often stark destitution. By the time some had succeeded in achieving a modest level of economic security, the Great Depression loomed. So Russian émigrés faced extraordinary hardships in the 1920s and 1930s. This dramatizes a number of fundamental questions about the relationship between the refugees and their hosts. How were the refugees received? How did they acquire the basics of life: shelter, food, clothing? How did they find employment? How did they satisfy their spiritual needs? To what extent did they assimilate?

GETTING OUT

Constantinople was the first stop for many who would eventually settle in Paris or New York. Passage through Constantinople came to symbolize the exile experience for Russians worldwide. Vera Lebedev, in her fictionalized account of White Russians in Detroit, describes the emotions aboard one of Wrangel's evacuation ships while the Crimean shoreline was rapidly fading from view. She notes the terrible silence: "No one, the people or the children, wept or talked or made so much as a motion. They stood there absolutely still, facing northeast toward Russia, like a shipload of robots in a dream." Then came the singing of the Orthodox hymn, "Lord have mercy on us," and finally everyone began to weep.[3] A Parisian-born daughter of refugees conjures up an image from her family lore: "Constantinople, the magic city to which they all fled and from which they all took off like sparrows, stateless and free, to settle at what they thought would be their final destination."[4]

A few well-connected upper-class Russians were able to proceed directly on to western Europe, frequently aboard British or French naval vessels. British and French warships regularly called at Russian Black Sea ports during the 1918-1920 allied intervention in support of the Whites against the Reds. So it came about that the Grand Duke Alexander was carried from Russia in January 1919 on the English cruiser *H.M.S. Forsythe*. A second cousin of Tsar Nicholas, the grand duke made his way to Paris where he had kept an apartment before the war.[5] One of the tsar's nieces, the ethereally beautiful Irene Yusupov, and her husband, Félix, were also picked up from the Crimean shore by a British ship. Prince Félix was one of the conspirators who had murdered the infamous Rasputin, the prince himself having fired a bullet into the monk's body after poison apparently failed to take effect. Nicholas II exiled Félix to one of his estates in central Russia, thus removing him from Bolshevik strongholds; and possibly saving that rash young man's life. The British conveyed the Yusupovs to Malta. Félix sold family jewels in order to continue the journey to Italy, London, and finally Paris. The Yusupov Parisian residence, decorated with flamboyant originality by the prince himself, became a regular gathering place for diverse company. An odd assortment of émigrés and internationals frequented the seemingly endless succession of Yusupov soirees.[6]

Evgraf Kovalevsky had been a prominent education official in the Imperial Russian government. His family found places on the Russian ship *Alexander III*, which departed from Constantinople in February 1920. The nineteen-year-old son, Peter, recorded that the ship was very clean and everywhere displayed the Imperial Russian symbol, the double-headed eagle. There were twenty French and 100 Russian passengers aboard. While they were still in the Sea of Marmara one of the Russian women suffered a mental breakdown. At supper she suddenly became distraught, distractedly combed at her hair, and then began to disrobe. She had to be forcibly restrained. The rest of the week's voyage passed without incident, and the Kovalevskys disembarked at Marseilles. They soon settled into an apartment in Nice.[7]

The family of Prince Ilarion Wassiltchikov sailed from the Crimean aboard an English warship. The prince had been a Duma member and Marshal of the Nobility (an official elected by noblemen in a given province as their representative). After several years in Baden-Baden the family moved to Paris. A daughter, Tatiana, eventually married Prince Paul Metternich (great-grandson of the famous Austrian chancellor), and they survived the Second World War to restore their Johannisberg castle and vineyards on the banks of the Rhine.[8]

Many Russians who took the Bosporus exodus were dropped in Constantinople and forced to eke out a living there while awaiting further opportunities. Possibly embellishing the facts, Natalia Malenevsky tells a dramatic adventure story. Her family barely escaped the Red occupation of Odessa in 1919 because of their friendship with General Sovkine of the White Army. They boarded an old Russian cargo ship with the general's family, passed through a storm, and landed on the Turkish coast near the Bosporus. English troops picked them up and provided phenol baths to kill typhus-bearing vermin. Arriving at Prinkipo Island near Constantinople, Natalia recalls devouring twelve oranges and three large chocolate bars with apparently no ill effects. When they found accommodations in Constantinople, Natalia disguised herself as a boy and thus obtained work from a local wool merchant. She then became a secretary for the American Red Cross and by examination won an educational stipend from the American Committee for Relief of Russian Refugees. This gave her the right to a French entry visa which she acquired for the purpose of studying medicine in Paris.[9]

Nina Don made the same journey that year in several stages. Alone and pregnant, she was first carried aboard the French cruiser *Du Chayla*, from Nikolaev to Odessa. Eventually she was able to link up with her husband, a naval officer, and the couple with their newborn daughter were evacuated to Constantinople by the Russian navy. Nina's husband and his fellow officers received six months of severance pay which was a considerable benefit.[10]

Usually Constantinople was only the first of several sojourns along the path of exile. Dr. Boris Alexandrovsky was initially awestruck by the immensity of the Wrangel evacuation: "As the ships plied the waves, bodies of those dead from wounds or typhus were confined to the deep. Babies were born.[11] He continued medical service with the White veterans at the Gallipoli camp for nine months, moved on to Bulgaria where he maintained a medical practice for five years, and then shifted to France for a twenty-one year stint before finally repatriating to the U.S.S.R.[12]

White Army veteran, Serge Rubakine, also spent nine months at the Gallipoli camp. He lived somewhat less than five years in Bulgaria as an agricultural laborer, then he too shifted to France. Traversing the country several times, he worked as a longshoreman, steel worker, miner, dishwasher, and member of a railroad section gang. Reaching Paris he was employed by the Renault automobile plant, then by the metro system, and at last he settled down as a taxi driver. In the meantime he had married a French woman and was raising three children.[13]

Similarly checkered adventures befell Emmanuel Soyfer. He and his family were all stricken by typhus in the Black Sea coastal town of Novorossisk in 1919, and his mother died in the epidemic. The survivors got visas from the local French Military Mission, and in March 1920, were transported to a French camp in the vicinity of Constantinople. Sleeping temporarily on the crowded floor of a seminary refectory, they did achieve some respite through the delicious ragouts prepared by the camp cook, a Senegalese sergeant in the French army. For about a year the father and two sons rented a room from a Greek in Constantinople and supported themselves mainly by selling off the deceased mother's wardrobe. Then the brothers were enrolled in a French "college" in Varna, Bulgaria. Emmanuel obtained a diploma in pharmacy. In 1930 he went to France, taking a job as director of a chemical plant. He married a Frenchwoman, and they had a son. His brother arrived in France in 1936, and during the Second World War they both fought in the French resistance movement.[14]

Mothers and children frequently made their escapes without the company of men. In 1920 Lisa Skobtzova was in Tiflis, in the Georgian Caucasus. She paid an enormous bribe to the maid of a railroad executive and got herself, her mother, and two children by rail to British-controlled Batum. From there they sailed to Constantinople and joined Lisa's husband. They all spent a winter in Yugoslavia and went on to Paris in 1922. Lisa Skobtzova later became a nun and as Mother Marie was prominent in the Parisian Russian colony for her charitable works.[15]

Lydia Kniagevich passed through the most remarkable vicissitudes seeking haven for herself and her son, Dima. She was a widowed noblewoman who by April 1919, with the Bolsheviks only forty miles away, decided to flee her Crimean estate. A 7,000-ruble fee (about $3,500) secured passage on a Turkish cargo sailing vessel. They sailed at Easter midnight, three Turkish crewman and four passengers, on a twenty-foot yawl with neither hold nor deck. As Lydia remembers it, they had a close brush with a Bolshevik patrol boat, ran through a terrible thirty-hour storm, and on the seventh day reached Turkey. She and seventeen-year-old Dima worked a year in Batum as translators for the British Command.

Having procured French visas, they made their way to Beaulieu, between Nice and Monte Carlo. Lydia got a sum of money from a Swiss bank, deposited there by her late husband after the scare of the 1905 revolution. That did not last long, however, and she began to earn income through piano playing. She started with renditions of waltzes, fox-trots, and tangos, performing in local bars and hotels and the occasional sumptuous villa. She began to accompany Mme Sedova, Russian prima ballerina of the former Petersburg Imperial Ballet Company. That led to requests for lessons which in turn led to her meeting the American singer Oscar Seagle. He invited her to be coach and accompanist for a four-month season at Schroon Lake in the Adirondacks. She immediately agreed. Some visa difficulties forced her and Dima to spend an extremely disagreeable three weeks on Ellis Island. Friends in the U.S.A. procured legal help for them though, and Congressman Sol Bloom who heard her at Schroon Lake secured Lydia a permanent visa. Dima was in good standing with his student visa. Lydia established a successful career in the U.S.A. as a piano recitalist.[16]

Refugees also crossed the western border of the Soviet Union at a great many points, usually by rail or on foot. Kiev, ancient capital of the Ukraine, changed hands nineteen times during the civil war, enduring occupations at different stages by Ukrainian factions, the German army, and Polish troops. In January 1919, the city was controlled by Ukrainian nationalists, and the Rzewuski family of Polish origins were able to slip away by train to Trieste. Alex Rzewuski proceeded to Florence, then to Paris. He enjoyed some artistic success as a painter until 1927 when he became a novice in the Dominican Order.[17]

Thousands of refugees found their ways to the West through Poland and Finland. Lev Liubimov recounts how his father, a senator of the Russian Empire, was held prisoner by the Soviet secret police, the Chekha, until many testimonials to his good character brought about his release. The family bribed a Communist Party official to authorize the former senator's train passage to Warsaw; this cost two "fine" Polenov paintings and a valuable early nineteenth century china service. (Lev notes that the venal official was soon after shot as an imposter and counterfeiter.) The next year, 1919, mother and son were able to obtain passports and took the train from Petrograd's Finland Station to Helsinki. They rejoined the father in Warsaw. Lev served briefly as a secretary for the Russian Diplomatic Mission in Bulgaria. After Wrangel's defeat, the family went to Berlin where Lev entered the university. In 1924 they moved to Paris, and Lev eventually became a journalist for the émigré paper, *Vozrozhdenie (Renaissance)*.[18]

Princess Sophia Volkonskaia walked into Finland in 1919. She describes crossing a bridge over a muddy stream and finding sanctuary in the town of Terioka. But she returned to Petrograd to join her husband. His family was originally Estonian, so they got permission in 1921 for train travel to Estonia. Later they settled in Paris.[19] Terioka is also named by S. Vladislavev as the first haven for him and his mother after they crossed the Finnish border. Then they went directly to Paris.[20]

Another young man who entered Finland in 1919 was Count Boris Berg. He disarmingly admits that "Naturally, I was completely confident that the situation would change and that my absence was only temporary. Was it then possible to suppose that I was parting forever from cherished, wonderful Petersburg and leaving forever all that was nearest and dearest to me?"[21] In Paris a year later he renewed his ties with a close family friend, Princess Golitsin. Berg was well connected socially; he was a nephew of Princess Yurevsky, the woman who had married morganatically Emperor Alexander II. Princess Golitsin persuaded Myron T. Herrick, American ambassador to France, to provide Boris with an American visa in 1922. It was a six-month tourist visa, but Berg stayed on for years illegally. By 1936, though, he was working for the Matchabelli perfumery and applied for his "first papers."[22]

A few lucky individuals were saved by intervention from the outside. Mikhail Osorgin, for example, benefited from his connection with inter-

national relief organizations. He had been an active member of the populist Socialist Revolutionary party, and during the civil war he served on
a Moscow committee to aid famine victims. According to Osorgin the
Committee was careful to avoid politics, but his group was independent,
and their success was an embarrassment to the Soviet government. Six of
the committee members including Osorgin were arrested and were to be
shot for counter-revolutionary activities. But League of Nations Refugee
Commissioner Fridtjof Nansen interceded and was able to save them.
Osorgin was expelled with that famous group of intellectuals in the
autumn of 1922.[23]

As is true in all great social catastrophes, children were the most pitiable
of victims. An émigré publication of 1920 lists the names of more than
1,000 child refugees in France, all originally from Petersburg. Some of
these lost one or both parents under horrifying circumstances: "Serezha
reported that 'The Bolsheviks shot Papa in Ekaterinoslav, and mama
hanged herself...'. Sonya explained that 'Papa died from typhus on the
steamer, and they threw him into the sea. Mama worked in a restaurant
but fell ill; they fired her'." French official figures show 656 Russian children in the Paris communal schools alone in 1923.[24] At decade's end an
émigré agency was still reporting the tragedies suffered by children:

> Alexandrine D., nine years old — brought in 1930 to a Polish hospital
> by fleeing Russian peasants. Her parents, Petrograd intellectuals,
> were killed while crossing the frontier. Alexander T., ten years old —
> The father, a prosperous market gardener, was deported to the North
> where he perished. During flight, mother fell under river ice but
> struggled on to the first Polish village where she collapsed and soon
> died (1930). Nicholas P., ten years old, Father had been a medical
> technician. While the family was fleeing, oldest son was killed by a
> Soviet patrol. Others hid in marsh. They all nearly drowned but
> reached Poland. The father immediately fell ill and died in several
> days. The mother survived but under the weight of her suffering lost
> her mind.[25]

The concern to educate such children and to instill in them a love for their
Russian heritage was a major preoccupation in the émigré community.

The Russian civil war embroiled a large group of Petrograd children in
a two-year round-the-world saga. In the summer of 1918 a committee of
parents sent more than 1,000 of their children with teachers into the countryside where food would be more plentiful. To escape the expanding
civil war, they moved farther and farther to the east beyond the Urals.
Clashes between Bolshevik forces and Czech Legionnaires along the
Trans-Siberian Railroad cut off any possibility of return to Petrograd. By
the end of the year a Siberian Commission of the American Red Cross
accepted the request of local Russian authorities to take most of these
children in its charge. Soon the White Kolchak government based in
Omsk collapsed, the Reds were advancing, and the Red Cross moved its
charges to the safety of Vladivostok. There they remained with a number

of Russian Red Cross nurses who joined them until July 1920. Then the Red Cross chartered a Japanese ship to carry them home via Japan, San Francisco, the Panama Canal, New York, and Finland.

On 28 August 1920, the Red Cross contingent of 780 children landed in the port of New York. During their two-week visit they attracted a great deal of attention and controversy. They were housed at Fort Wadsworth on Staten Island and received many visitors, mostly Russian immigrants. The pro- and anti-Soviet camps accused each other of damaging the children's best interests. Right-wing émigré spokesman, Boris Brasol, complained of a "gang of irresponsible internationalists,... the east side Bolsheviki," who were preaching "anarchy and corruption" to the children. A pro-Soviet rally including Norman Thomas was held at Madison Square Garden. Speakers protested that the Red Cross was planning to land the children in France, a place they did not want to stop because it was an enemy of the Soviet Union. (The Red Cross was considering a French stopover, but that proved unnecessary.)

During their stay the children enjoyed extensive sightseeing of the city and a meeting with the mayor. President and Mrs. Wilson sent them a letter and an autographed photo of the presidential couple for each child. A benefit concert was held for them in Madison Square Garden, sponsored by fifty local Russian societies. The money went to buy them clothing and gifts, including musical instruments. (Some of the children were anxious to play the American music they were hearing.) At Fort Wadsworth the Russian children hosted thousands of American Girl Scouts. The Russian Girl Scout Band played and seventy Russian Girl Scouts put on an exhibition drill. But on two occasions, groups of boys, about 175 in all, broke out of Fort Wadsworth and scattered without permission. The police called it a "Bolshevist plot." Red Cross officials saw it as "a boyish desire to roam about the city." In any case they were all eventually rounded up.

The children were anxious to remain together until they returned "home." One boy characteristically refused the offer of his aunt to stay with her family in Fall River, Massachusetts. Another, though, tragically never left American soil. Two days before sailing, one of the children was killed in a freak accident. While a soldier was demonstrating the manual of arms, his rifle discharged, instantly killing fifteen-year-old Pavel Nikolaeff. The boy was buried the following day in Mount Olivet Cemetery in Queens. Early next morning all the rest of the "globe circling waifs" embarked once more. Ultimately, forty of the children were delivered to parents living outside the U.S.S.R. and the rest were repatriated to Petrograd.[26]

A considerable number of others who went through Siberia were consciously seeking escape from the Soviet regime. One large group that had gathered in the Pacific port of Vladivostok put to sea aboard fifteen small craft in the fall of 1922. They made stops in Korea and China, and several hundred remained in Shanghai, joining the already sizable Russian émigré colony there. The flotilla worked its way down to Sumatra, lost one vessel and some crew in a storm, and then altered course for the Philippines where it finally landed in Manila Bay.[27]

The American Red Cross and the War Department arranged for 526 of the refugees to be carried to San Francisco on the army transport ship *Merritt*. When the *Merritt* docked on 1 July 1928, the Russian Refugee Relief Society of America took the passengers in hand. The San Francisco Chamber of Commerce called together heads of large firms, and jobs were found for the newcomers throughout the northern part of the state, in the lumber industry, box factories, and fruit picking. C.W. Riley, who coordinated the settlement effort, reported to the Red Cross that fall that "both employers and the refugees express great satisfaction."[28]

NEW YORK AND PARIS IN THE TWENTIES

The largest and best organized refugee communities in the United States and France were a group of 6,000 in New York City and 50,000 in Paris. Emigré intellectual and cultural activities were concentrated in these two extraordinarily dynamic cities. Entering the 1920s New York and Paris both began to shake off the numbing effects of the Great War, each with its own characteristic exuberance.

New York's modernist movement in the arts was centered in Greenwich Village. Theodore Dreiser and Sherwood Anderson lived close by one another on St. Luke's Place. Willa Cather presided over her Friday afternoon teas at 5 Bank Street. Noel Coward stopped for a time on Macdougal Street. Edmund Wilson, then managing editor of *The New Republic*, was also a Village resident. Thomas Wolfe lived there too, brooding in isolation. In 1921, there was an exodus to Paris. Malcolm Cowley, e.e. cummings, John Dos Passos, and Edna St. Vincent Millay made the pilgrimage, seeking fresh inspiration in what was undoubtedly the artistic center of European-American culture. But by 1923 they were all back in the Village, for as authors Susan Edmiston and Linda D. Cirino put it, "They found European artists and intellectuals more defeated and demoralized than those at home...."[29] Poets Marianne Moore and Hart Crane were Villagers. Eugene O'Neill was still there, having been one of the moving spirits in establishing the Provincetown Playhouse on Macdougal Street. That helped stimulate the "Little Theater Movement" which was spreading rapidly across the country. Accompanying the literary creativity, more serious painting and sculpture was being produced in Greenwich Village than elsewhere in the United States.

In Midtown, the Round Table was becoming an institution at the Algonquin Hotel. There gathered Alexander Woollcott, Franklin P. Adams, Heywood Broun, Robert Sherwood, Robert Benchley, Dorothy Parker, Edna Ferber, George F. Kaufman, Marc Connelly, and Harold

Ross, all of whom did much to establish the hard-boiled, wisecracking, cynical tone of the twenties.

Uptown the Harlem Renaissance was underway, a relatively genteel exploration of African-American identity by the "Talented Tenth." Its foremost spokesmen were poets Countee Cullen and Langston Hughes. Along 125th Street and in the adjacent neighborhood of Sugar Hill many creative figures, people like Paul Robeson and W.E.B. Du Bois, were producing the most exciting decade in Harlem's history.

New York offered much, but a good number of Americans preferred Paris. In fact, the largest American colony in Europe was settled there. Gertrude Stein held court in her studio apartment near the Luxembourg Gardens. Nearby in the Latin Quarter was Sylvia Beach's Shakespeare and Company, where English and American books could be bought or borrowed. Close at hand were Ernest Hemingway, Ezra Pound, and Archibald MacLeish. Djuna Barnes, haughty and inscrutable, convinced everyone that she was a brilliant writer. For a time the Scott Fitzgeralds lived over by the Etoile. Fitzgerald and Hemingway first discussed the newly published *Great Gatsby* in the Closerie des Lilas café, on Boulevard Montparnasse.

Englishmen ranging from George Orwell to Wyndham Lewis came and went. James Joyce could often be seen dining with his family at the elegant Michaud's Restaurant. Among the French avant-garde, Surrealism reached its high point in the early twenties. André Breton, Louis Aragon, and Jean Cocteau were prominent in the movement.

On a more popular level, "going to the movies" now became a major form of mass entertainment, and the powerful American movie-making industry dominated the international markets. Douglas Fairbanks and Charlie Chaplin (known in Europe as Charlot) were the reigning stars on both sides of the Atlantic. Lillian Gish, Gloria Swanson, Mary Pickford, and many other stars were just as well known in Paris as in New York. French film makers reflected the artistic ferment of Paris and made their contributions to the development of film technique. Abel Gance was outstanding within the impressionist school of directors for the originality and grandeur of his conceptions.

The popularity of films was an aspect of the new society being created by mass production and mass marketing after the First World War. Increasing commercialization could be seen even in the changing physical aspects of towns and cities. Luxurious residences of the wealthy, occupying highly valued real estate sites, were being demolished and replaced by banks, insurance companies, business offices, luxury stores, fashionable theaters, and restaurants. This was happening in New York along Fifth Avenue and in Paris up and down the Champs-Elysées.

The most salient feature of life in the United States in the twenties was the noble experiment of Prohibition. As the puritanical mood of wartime lifted, the public proved unable to contain its thirst for alcohol, and a new type of nightclub or "speakeasy" appeared to fill the need. There were eventually some 9,000 of these illegal operations in New York City alone. The better clubs were restaurants which featured dance teams and served a restricted, exclusive membership. French names were popular, suggesting Gallic abandon: the Palais Royal (featuring Paul Whiteman for a time), Moulin Rouge, Bal Tabirin, Beaux Arts Café, Montmartre, and Monte Carlo. Among the smart clubs with good restaurants were the Mirador (where the Russian Fokine Ballet once performed), the Moritz, and the Deauville. The Club Intime, presided over by the most ebullient of hostesses, Texas Guinan, was one of the most expensive, with cover charges ranging upwards from $20. Of course that afforded one the opportunity to watch Ruby Keeler dancing. Texas maintained a quiet home with her husband on Eighth Street amidst the Greenwich Village artists. At the Trocadero Club Fred and Adele Astaire performed. Especially lively night life was to be found in Harlem. Some spots catered to whites, although others refused to admit them. One for whites only was the fabulous Cotton Club, white-owned, with a "high yaller" chorus line and featuring such greats as Cab Calloway and Duke Ellington. People were learning to dance the Lindy Hop, the Charleston and the Black Bottom. Men and women, black and white, were mixing in the New York clubs, eating, drinking, dancing, and smoking, to an unprecedented degree for "respectable" Americans.

Similar diversions were part of the Paris scene although not quite so novel there. The Parisian café still was the typical meeting place where one could drink spirits or coffee, have a meal or not, and enjoy one's friends in a relaxed atmosphere. Artistic types favored the Montparnasse cafés, the Rotonde, the Sélect, and, across the boulevard, the Dôme, which was the most frequented by the American colony. Another favorite gathering place was the Deux Magots, on the Boulevard Saint-Germain. Near the Opéra was Harry's New York Bar, where the Bloody Mary and Sidecar cocktails were invented. In the *bals musettes* of the Latin Quarter, one might dance the new fox trot or java. And Paris soon knew the Charleston and the Black Bottom. One heard the same songs in the clubs and cabarets of New York and Paris: "Ramona," "Three O'Clock in the Morning," "I'm Just Wild About Harry," "Charleston," "The Man I Love," and "Let's Do It."

Cole Porter became a Parisian in this period. After living at the Ritz, he and his glamorous wife Linda moved into a beautiful house at 13 rue Monsieur, not far from the Hotel des Invalides. Among their friends were the Scott Fitzgeralds, Michael Arlen, the John Barrymores, Serge Diaghilev, and Serge Lifar. They often met at Bricktop's night-club. Bricktop, the African-American owner, named for her red hair, was a celebrity in her own right. Cole Porter wrote a song for her, "Miss Otis Regrets, She is Unable to Lunch Today."

Josephine Baker, Baltimore born and bred, burst upon the Paris scene in the spectacular La Revue Nègre which opened on the Champs-Elysées. She first appeared adorned with a single pink Flamingo feather. Parisian audiences took her to their hearts and elevated her to the pinnacle of stardom which had formerly been occupied by Mistinguett.

Undoubtedly the best known of all Americans living ab‑‑‑ ‑d was Isadora Duncan, she who had been midwife to the modern dance. She gave Sunday night suppers in her house on the rue de la Pompe "where guests strolled in, strolled out, and from low divans supped principally on champagne and strawberry tarts, while Isadora, barely clad in chiffon robes, rose when the spirit moved her to dance exquisitely."[30]

This was the "Jazz Age," the "Roaring Twenties,"a time of unparalleled social change, especially in New York. In both cities the arts were in ferment, and creative people were fundamentally reevaluating traditional standards and beliefs. The values which had permitted the catastrophe of the First World War were now repudiated. The nineteenth century was finally ended, and the twentieth century was being born. Gertrude Stein observed, "Paris was where the twentieth century was." And John Jay Chapman had written, even before the war, "The present in New York is so powerful that the past is lost."

A very few Russian émigrés participated fully in this ferment, those like the Prince and Princess Yusupov and Igor Stravinsky in Paris, or, André Kostelanetz and Igor Sikorsky in New York. But the great majority of Russian émigrés inhabited an entirely different Paris and New York. These cities for them were havens to cherish the past rather than the future.

NOTES TO INTRODUCTION

1. For an overview of the diaspora, see John J. Stephan, *The Russian Fascists — Tragedy and Farce in Exile , 1925-1945* (NY, 1978), pp. 1-15, 31-47. On Harbin, see Simon Karlinsky, "Memoirs of Harbin," *Slavic Review* 48 (Summer 1989): 284-290.

2. M. Osharov, "To Alien Shores: The 1922 Expulsion of Intellectuals from the Soviet Union," *Russian Review* 32 (July 1973): 295-297.

3. Vera Lebedeff, *The Heart Returneth* (Philadelphia, 1943), 169.

4. Natacha Stewart, "The Dacha," *New Yorker* (May 20, 1985), 39.

5. Alexander, Grand Duke of Russia, *Always A Grand Duke* (New York, 1933), 3, 4, 23.

6. Prince Félix Yousoupoff, *En exil ...* (Paris, 1954), 1-4.

7. *Diary* , Jan.-Feb., 1920, pp. 27-44, Petr E. Kovalevskii, Box 2, Bakhmeteff Archive, Coumbia University.

8. Tatiana Metternich, *Purgatory of Fools* (New York, 1976), 13, 26, 37, 285.

9. Natalia Malenevsky, *Les naufragés de la Mer Noire: histoire de malia, jeune fille russe* (Paris, 1978), 158-301.

10. *The Year 1919* , 5-25, Nina S. Don Memoirs, Box 1, Bakhmeteff Archive, Columbia University.

11. Boris N. Alexandrovsky, *Iz perezhitogo v chuzhikh kraiakh, vospominaniia i dumy byvshego emigranta (Experiences in Foreign Climes, Reminiscences and Thoughts of a Former Emigrant)* (Moscow, 1969), 17.

12. Ibid., 29, 51-67.

13. Jean Anglade, *La vie quotidienne des immigrés en France de 1919 à nos jours* (Paris, 1976), 17-25.

14. Emmanuel Soyfer, *40 ans après* (Monaco, 1969), 109-180.

15. T. Stratton Smith, *Mère Marie, nonne et rebelle* , trans. René Jouan (Paris, 1965), 111-117.

16. Lydia Kniagevitch, *Lights Vanished* (NY, 1940), 182-227.

17. Alex Rzewuski, *A travers l'invisible cristal : confessions d'un dominican* (Paris, 1976), 151-152.

18. Lev Liubimov, *Na Chuzhbine (In a Foreign Land)* (Moscow, 1963), 88-121, 159.

19. Kniaginia Sof'ia Volkonskaia, *Gore pobezhdennym, vae victis, vospominaiia (Woe to the Vanquished, Memoirs)* (Paris, ca. 1932), 7-12, 160.

20. S. Vladislavlev (pseud. S-. Kamenskii), *Iz zapisnoi knizhki bezhentsa (From a Refugee's Notebook)* (Paris, 1963), 12-17.

21. *Vospominaniia Gr. B. G. Berga (posle litseia)*, typescript, 138, B. G. Berg, Box 3 Bakhmeteff Archive, Columbia University.

22. Ibid., 156-164.

23. Mikhail Osorgin, *Saisons*, Any Barda & Sylvie Técoutoff (Lausanne, 1973), 171-174.

24. Tatiana Aleksinskaia, "Emigratsiia in ee molodoe polkolenie" ("The Emigration and its young People"), *Zvozrozhdenia (Renaissance)*, Paris monthly,65 (May, 1957): 20-21.

25. *Question d'aide aux enfants, nouveaux réfugiés russes*, extracts from Zemgor reports, ca. 1933, Association pour la conservation des valeurs culturelles russes, 1917-1947, 8 AS, 137, Archives Nationales, Paris.

26. Foster Rhea Dulles, *The American Red Cross — A History* (New York, 1950), 212. *New York Times* , daily stories (August 31 - September 12, 1920). Floyd Miller, *The Wild Children of the Urals* (New York, 1965), 175-214.

27. W. Chapin Huntington, *The Homesick Million, Russia-out-of-Russia* (Boston, 1933), 15-17.

28. Philippines, *Refugees in ... evacuated to the United States* , Russia WWI, 948.62, American National Red Cross Archives, Washington, D.C. See also *New York Times* (July 2, 1923), 16 and (July 3, 1923), 2.

29. Susan Edmiston and Linda D. Cirino, *Literary New York*, (Boston, 1976), 70.

30. Janet Flanner (Genêt), *Paris Was Yesterday* ed. Irving Drutman (New York, 1972), 31.

II. The League of Nations and Fridtjof Nansen

As hundreds of thousands fled the Russian revolution and the civil war, most without means or destination, governments tried to block their entry. Philanthropic agencies such as the International Red Cross were overwhelmed by the magnitude of the relief effort required. One hundred seventy thousand Russians in Constantinople needed food and shelter. Appeals to do something for the refugees inundated the newly-created League of Nations, and in the second year of its existence, 1921, the League appointed Dr. Fridtjof Nansen to be High Commissioner for Refugees.

Fridtjof Nansen was a famous Norwegian polar explorer who enjoyed immense international prestige. He had led a team of six men who were the first to cross Greenland, from east to west coast, on skis. In 1895, he and a single companion made a dash for the North Pole. They had to turn back about 275 miles short of their goal, but they had advanced considerably farther north than any before them. Not only was Nansen renowned for his physical courage as a polar explorer, but he was acclaimed for his scientific contributions in the fields of zoology and oceanography. He entered the realm of international politics when he was instrumental in helping Norway to achieve independence from Sweden in 1905. For more than two years Nansen served as ambassador to Great Britain for the newly independent Norway. These experiences increased his prestige, for he was recognized as a statesman of exceptional integrity and humanitarianism. He was a strong supporter of the League of Nations and a prominent international figure as the First World War drew to a close.

The League called upon Nansen to direct the repatriation of war prisoners. When he undertook this task in May 1920, he calculated that there were 300,000 such prisoners still on Soviet territory.[1] Soviet authorities would not cooperate with the League which had blackballed them, but they were willing to work with Nansen on an unofficial basis. Nansen had traveled extensively in Russia and had written sympathetically of the Russian people, which helped him gain the confidence of the Bolsheviks. He used his personal prestige to raise the necessary funds and to coordinate the work of agencies like the International Red Cross and YMCA and he successfully organized a series of prisoner exchanges. His efficiency in the repatriation of war prisoners and his entrée with Soviet officialdom made Nansen the natural choice to be High Commissioner for Refugees. Practically all "refugees" in 1921 were people in flight from the Soviet regime.

Before he could turn his attention to refugees, however, Nansen was asked by charitable organizations to take charge of relief operations for famine-stricken Russia. Russian writer Maxim Gorky personally appealed to Nansen to help save starving Russians. A devastating famine exacerbated by the civil war gripped the Russian land by 1921. That year the harvest was a complete failure in the most fertile regions of the country, the Volga river basin and the southern Ukraine. The League of Nations could not bring itself to agree to any form of aid for "Bolsheviks," and vociferous Russian exile groups in Paris also opposed famine relief because it would help prop up the Soviet regime. So Nansen again acted essentially on his own. He obtained contributions from many private and semi-official sources. The American Relief Administration under Herbert Hoover was immensely helpful. Nansen wrote, "In the whole history of the world there is no humanitarian work that can be compared with the relief work organized by Hoover during and after the War, which had its climax here in Russia."[2] In the end Nansen's endeavor saved about 12,000,000 people. At least 3,000,000 died.[3]

While his efforts to aid famine victims yet continued, Nansen took up the problems of Russian refugees. The main task with which he was charged as high commissioner was to find employment for the refugees. No funds were provided by the League to establish or subsidize productive enterprises. Nansen would have to persuade governments to accept refugees into their own work forces. He found that the greatest obstacle to job placement was the general economic crisis in Europe following the war. Millions of former soldiers were now seeking civilian jobs, war industries had to be converted to peacetime uses, and the political map of Europe had been redrawn, causing economic chaos. Faced with these tremendous challenges, harried officials were not much concerned with non-citizens. In 1922 Nansen believed that the ultimate solution of the Russian refugee problem would be repatriation. But he noted in his first major report to the League that "the present ravages of famine and disease preclude this now."[4] For the time being, Nansen was going to have to rely on the largess of governments and private relief agencies. His role would be that of a coordinator and facilitator.

The high commissioner appointed his own representatives to act for refugees in those countries where they were concentrated. The greatest number were Russians, but he was occupied with other groups too, such as Greeks and Assyrians. He persuaded the concerned governments to name special officials who were charged as liaisons with Nansen and his representatives. In France, for example, Nansen appointed M. Hainglaise to be his spokesman, and the Russian department of the Ministry for Foreign Affairs was the government liaison. By September of 1922, Nansen was able to report that his representatives in some countries had taken censuses of refugees, helped them secure visas, helped them find employment, and had coordinated the work of charitable organizations.

He noted the particular success in France of voluntary labor exchanges, established by the refugees themselves and supported Nansen's office.[5] It was becoming apparent that France was the one European country with significant employment opportunities.

Ten percent of the French active male population had been killed in the war; more had been incapacitated. Once the wrenching economic adjustments necessitated by the war's end had taken place, a serious manpower shortage was evident. Large-scale industrial and agricultural enterprises began to recruit foreign labor. During the twenties, 2,0000,000 immigrants came into France, and among them were hundreds of thousands of Russian refugees. Nansen reported, "without being accused of exaggeration, one can state that every Russian refugee able and willing to work in the capacity of an agricultural, industrial or manual worker can find in France remunerative employment. On the other hand, one can observe, especially during the last period, a pronounced movement towards France of the Russians, living in Germany, Austria, the Balkan countries and even in Russia itself."[6] True, there was work available in France, but it was generally menial labor of the most onerous kind. Such jobs were usually to be found in the provinces, far from Paris where the Russian émigrés were concentrated.

The greatest benefit that Nansen provided Russian refugees was his creation of the "Nansen Certificate." Commonly called the "Nansen passport," this was an identity card, recognized throughout Europe, in the absence of any other form of national identification. U.S. immigration officials accepted it. A Soviet decree of 1921 deprived practically all Russian refugees of nationality. It specifically renounced "Persons who voluntarily served in the armies fighting the Soviet regime, or who participated in counter-revolutionary organizations."[7] In any case, the typical émigré had left without papers or with passports issued by the defunct imperial government, and all of these people were now stateless. The League of Nations defined a "Russian" or "Nansen" refugee as "any person of Russian origin who does not enjoy or who no longer enjoys the protection of the Government of the Union of Socialist Soviet Republics and who has not acquired another nationality."[8]

Beginning in 1922, the League offered its protection to such persons by providing Nansen certificates. These were issued by individual governments and were valid for one year only. They were not comparable to standard national passports. During the twenties no government allowed a certificate holder to leave the country and return automatically. Nevertheless, the Nansen certificate did lend to its holder something of a sense of identity, gave him various kinds of legal protection from the League, did allow for the possibility of travel, and eased the way to obtaining a work permit. For his many exertions on behalf of the distressed, Nansen won the Nobel Peace Prize in 1922. He donated all the money to refugee causes.

In 1926, the high commissioner with the League's backing persuaded a number of European governments to issue special stamps, to be affixed to refugee identity certificates. Those who had the means paid five Swiss gold francs (about $1 at that time) for this "Nansen stamp." The indigent were issued stamps gratis. Proceeds from stamps sold were used for refugee relief. Thus, the Nansen stamp was a means whereby better-off refugees helped to support their less fortunate fellows.

In 1923, Nansen's efforts to arrange for repatriation of émigrés by the Soviet government came to an end. Soviet intransigence, exemplified by their denationalization of most exiles, the objection of almost all refugees to repatriation, and wide acceptance of the Nansen certificate combined to keep the refugees in permanent exile. Those most in need of help were the vast number jammed into Constantinople. The bulk of soldiers from the White Army were resettled in Bulgaria and Yugoslavia, where they worked on farms, built roads, worked in mines, and served as frontier guards. With Nansen's aid, several thousand persons were transferred form Constantinople to France.

In 1922 and 1923, 1,771 Russians went from Constantinople to France; 2,041 went from Constantinople to the United States. About 100 Russian orphans were placed with French agricultural families by the *Placement Familial*. The entire Russian Red Cross Orphanage in Constantinople, consisting of 100 children and 20 adults, was transferred to Namur in France. Nansen provided 18,000 French francs to finance the transfer. With the help of the American Red Cross and the American Relief Administration, funds and transportation were provided to the United States. There the Russian Refugee Relief Society of America took charge. Immigrants pledged to repay sums that had been advanced to them, and that money went to the Russian Refugee Relief Society.[9]

By the end of 1923 there were perhaps 8,000 Russians still residing in Constantinople, and most heads of families had found employment. It seemed the group had come through the worst and could fend for itself. But allied military authorities transferred power to the Ataturk government, and the Turkish and Soviet republics quickly recognized one another. In January 1924, Turkish authorities handed over the Russian Embassy and Consulate in Constantinople to Soviet representatives. Militant Turkish nationalists suppressed Russian émigré organizations, restaurants, pharmacies, and other enterprises. Russian physicians and lawyers were barred from practice. Once again, Russian refugees in Constantinople became wholly dependent upon the protection of the high commissioner. Over the next few years many individual Russians and small groups continued to leave Turkey with the aid of the League.[10]

In January 1925, the International Labor Organization, associated with the League of Nations, assumed responsibility for transportation, settlement, and employment of refugees. Nansen as high commissioner handled political and legal aspects of the refugee problem. The ILO placed some 60,000 Russian refugees in jobs, for the most part in France. The

French Ministry of Agriculture cooperated to settle 2,000 *métayers* (share-croppers), most of whom were Cossacks that had experience in farm work.[11]

Nansen died in 1930, and the League created the "Nansen International Office for Refugees" to carry on his work. All League services for refugees, including job procurement, were brought together in this office. One of the major activities of the Nansen Office was intercession on behalf of refugees who were threatened with expulsion from the country that was harboring them. With the coming of depression and massive unemployment, refugees were increasingly subject to expulsion in order to reserve scarce jobs for citizens. Formerly hospitable France now turned xenophobic.

The depression reached France relatively late, but during the 1930s the French government more and more frequently resorted to expulsion orders. Minor infractions: "vagrancy or lack of money or work; delay in putting their papers in order or in paying the tax on their identity cards; working without authorization" could subject a refugee to expulsion.[12] "Working without authorization" particularly became a frequent cause of expulsion proceedings. In practice, there was usually no other country willing to receive an expellee, and he would then be imprisoned in France for six months. Upon release, again failing to leave the country, they would be reimprisoned. Vasily A. Maklakov, chief spokesman for the Russian émigrés in France, cited a case of one person thus incarcerated for ten years.[13] In 1934-1935, the Nansen Office interceded in France on behalf of 1,596 Russians subject to expulsion orders. As many as 4,000 may have had expulsion orders standing against them at that time.[14] The cost of imprisonment and pleas of the League led the French government to curtail this practice in the later 1930s. But the expulsion orders again proliferated during the increasingly tense year of 1939.[15]

Nansen and his League successors explored the possibilities in Latin America for employment and settlement of Russian refugees. About 3,000 were placed in Argentina, Brazil, Paraguay, Chile, and Mexico. Latin America seemed to most, however, remote and forbidding. Work opportunities tended to be limited to hard labor, and relatively few Russians made the journey there. The ILO was short of funds for transport, and the whole operation was stymied by the depression.

The League of Nations was the most effective in aiding Russian refugees during its very first years of operation, 1921-1923. With the vigorous commitment of Fridtjof Nansen, hundreds of thousands were fed, clothed, and settled. The successes of the Nansen International Office for Refugees were recognized in 1938 when it received the Nobel Peace Prize. The Nansen Certificate and the Nansen Stamp continued to be extremely useful to the émigré community into the period of the Second World War. As time passed, though, the League encountered mounting difficulties in refugee assistance. The general depression of the thirties reduced employment and the funds of charitable organizations. Repeated failures to prevent international aggression during the same decade weakened the League's moral authority. With the Soviet Union's entry into the League in 1934, its delegates opposed any aid to the "White" emigration. Then came a flood of refugees from Nazi Germany and Franco's Spain, compounding the problem.

Fridtjof Nansen was the most dedicated friend that the refugees ever had. He undertook the work of prisoner exchange, famine relief, and refugee aid with a full-fledged commitment to alleviate human suffering. He took no salary for any of these labors. He founded an effective refugee aid organization that outlived him, and he established the basic principle that the international community is responsible for all those suffering in exile. Nansen's exertions exhausted him, and his death in 1930 deprived the émigré community of an extraordinarily compassionate and potent champion.

NOTES TO CHAPTER II

1. Nansen Report to the League of Nations, *New York Times*, Nov. 19, 1920, 3.

2. Jon Sorensen, *The Saga of Fridtjof Nansen* (New York, 1932), 297.

3. Many weakened by hunger actually died of typhus which was spread by infected lice. One of Nansen's Norwegian co-workers was bitten on the neck by a louse while distributing food in the Ukraine, but he survived. Had the louse been more virulent or Major Vidkun Quisling more susceptible, the history of Norway during World War II might have been quite different. See Sorensen, 295-298.

4. Fridtjof Nansen, *Russian Refugees : General Report on the Work Accomplished up to March 15, 1922* (League of Nations, C. 124.M.74.1922), 11.

5. "Nansen Report," *Official Journal*, (*OJ*) Extract No. 6 (League of Nations, Sept. 15, 1922), 4.

6. "Nansen Report," *OJ* (Sept. 4, 1923), 11.

7. Durward Sandifer, "Status under Soviet Law of American Citizens of Russian Origin, " *American Journal of International Law* 30 (Oct. 1-936): 627.

8. Jacques Vernant, *The Refugee in the Post-War World* , (New Haven, Ct, 1953), 54, fn. 1.

9. "Nansen Report," *OJ* , Extract No. 19 (July 7, 1923), 3. "Nansen Report," OJ (Sept. 4, 1923), 7 & 11.

10. "Nansen Report," *OJ* , Extract No. 25 (March 10, 1924), 2.

11. Tatiana Schaufuss, "The White Russian Refugees," *Annals of the American Academy of Political and Social Sciences* 203 (May 1939): 49.

12. Nansen International Office for Refugees, *Report of the Governing Body for the Year Ending June 30th, 1935* (XII.B. International Bureaux. 1935. XII.B.1), 19.

13. André Beucler, "Russes de France," *Revue de Paris* , Année 44, tome 2 (April 15, 1937): 891.

14. Nansen International Office for Refugees, *Report of... June 30th*, 1935, p. 23. Dorothy Thompson, *Refugees — Anarchy or Organization?* (New York, 1938), 39.

15. Nansen International Office for Refugees, *Report of the Governing Body for the Year Ending June 30th, 1938* (XII.B International Bureaux.1938 XII.B.2.), 5.

III. French Government and the Refugees

France and England during the nineteenth century were favored asylums for political refugees fleeing repressive regimes. Thus Russian and Polish exiles formed permanent communities in Paris and London which were periodically replenished whenever the Russian imperial government would lash out to stifle opposition. France's commitment to the principle of asylum was underscored by her gift to the United States of the Statue of Liberty, symbol of a land of refuge for the world's oppressed. After the First World War, France became the preeminent country of refuge in the Western world. More people found haven in France during the twenties than in any other country including the United States. French nationalism still encompassed the enlightened idea of universal fraternity, and this helped to create a relatively receptive climate for immigrants. Denis Brogan, an eminent and sensitive observer of French affairs, wrote about this period, "In the face of the rising tide of racial mysticism, France asserted that being French is a state of mind, not a mystical inheritance."[1]

The Russians were one group of many refugees in France. Others had fled from the territory of the former Russian Empire, such as Poles, Ukrainians, and Georgians. There were a large group of Armenians and a smaller number of Turks in France, as well as a few Portuguese, Assyrians, and Assyro-Chaldeans. With the rise of Fascism came Italians, Spaniards, and Saarlanders. Germans and Jews fled the Nazi regime. In all, there was a net immigration into France of some 1,113,000 heads of households plus their families from 1921 to 1935.[2] Roughly 200,000 of these were Russians.

A declining birthrate and labor shortages had been serious concerns for the French government for half a century. From the 1800s France had been dependent upon imported foreign labor, and her tragic manpower losses during the Great War increased the need. Several million guest workers, mostly Italians and Poles, augmented the French labor force. In addition, the French ministries of Labor and Agriculture facilitated the entry of able-bodied refugees into France during the twenties. The government opened recruiting bureaus where exiles were most numerous, and visas and transportation were provided for those recruited. Refugee relief agencies faced a formidable task in helping hundred of thousands of homeless people to establish new lives after the First World War. Had it not been for the opportunities in France, that task would have been absolutely impossible. League of Nations' reports throughout the twenties confirm that all Russian refugees willing to work were able to find employment in France. Labor was needed especially in heavy industry, mines, mills, and construction work. The Ministry of Agriculture placed thousands as sharecroppers, an occupation particularly favored by the Cossacks.

The desire to increase her military manpower also caused France to encourage immigration. The German population was nearly double that of France and was rapidly increasing during the interwar period. Russians who clearly had no allegiance to the Soviet regime would be welcomed to make France their new *patrie* which their young men would be bound to defend with their lives. The wary French generally assumed that any future war would be with Germany, and it would be better to have Russian émigrés fighting on the French side rather than with the Germans.

Youth were most welcome, as potential soldiers or producers of soldiers. The French agency *Placement Familial* arranged for several hundred Russian orphans to find homes with French families, generally those of farmers. The government also provided educational aid to refugee children. Responding to the first great wave of Russian émigrés, the French Assembly in 1923 voted a credit of 450,000 francs ($25,000) to create educational scholarships for some 200 students.[3] Refugee children were admitted to the French public schools on an equal basis with French children.

The French government cooperated closely with the League of Nations regarding émigrés, specifically with the High Commissioner for Refugees. Nansen's representative in Paris continually worked with the Russian department of the French Foreign Ministry on refugee matters. French courts recognized the authority of Nansen's representative to legalize refugee documents, and he had the right to intercede on behalf of émigrés in court cases. In sum, the Nansen representative in France held a quasi-consular position that empowered him to defend the interests of Russian refugees.

The French government in 1925 also granted official status to the so-called " *Offices russes* ." These were successors to the prewar Russian diplomatic offices and were staffed by the same personnel. The Central Office in Paris, successor to the Russian Embassy, continued to be directed by Vasily A. Maklakov. Maklakov had been a prominent member of the last Imperial Duma (Council), and the Provisional Government of 1917 offered him the ambassadorship in Paris. At first he resisted, percipiently believing the government to be weak and ineffectual. But toward the end of summer 1917, still against his better judgment, he agreed to accept the post. Maklakov related what happened next, "The day that I presented myself at the Quai d'Orsay in order to deliver my credentials, M. Barthou informed me that Kerensky's government had been overthrown."[4] His doubts and hesitation were thus fully justified. Maklakov's credentials became null and void, and he was never officially recognized as an ambassador. He nonetheless resided in the Russian Embassy for the next seven years, and he was treated as an ambassador who had not yet been accredited. Maklakov wryly noted, "I resembled a magazine that one puts on a seat to show that it is occupied."[5] The Soviets took permanent possession of the seat in 1924.

France granted diplomatic recognition to the U.S.S.R. in October, 1924, and Soviet Ambassador Leonid Krassin took over the Russian Embassy on the rue de Grenelle. Since the Communist government had stripped refugees of their citizenship, there could be no relations between Soviet officials and stateless Russians.

The French government consequently faced the problem of dealing with tens of thousands of Russian émigrés, now "non-persons" in the view of Soviet diplomats. These émigrés did not wish to become naturalized French citizens: they were still loyal Russians by their own lights. Their papers were in Russian, and French officials for the most part would be unable to verify their documents or to understand their problems. It was thus decided that the former diplomatic personnel could best serve as intermediaries between the French government and the émigré colony. The Central Office in Paris carried on under Maklakov, and *Offices russes* in Marseilles and Nice maintained the work of the former Russian consulates there. These offices did what the Soviet Embassy would not do.

Maklakov and his associates settled various questions of civil status for refugees and attested to signatures and translations. In general, the offices drew up documents for refugees and verified data concerning them. By confirming these acts, the Nansen representative gave them legal force. As an example of the services rendered, the *Offices russes* certified all marriages contracted by the Russian émigrés. The offices dealt with questions of French policy affecting the émigré colony, they maintained neutrality in political matters, and they enjoyed authority in French official circles.

The *Offices russes* fulfilled their mandate in large part because of Vasily Maklakov. A sophisticated "European" in outlook, very well educated, he was celebrated for his brilliant speeches in the Imperial Duma. He had been part of the moderate liberal Duma opposition, a lawyer by profession. During his seven years as "unaccredited" ambassador to France, Maklakov showed genuine diplomatic skill in mediating among the sharply divided factions of the Russian colony. As long as he presided over the Russian embassy in Paris, he had the use of limited funds, money on hand for intelligence and propaganda work, the proceeds from the sale of surplus supplies and embassy properties in France. There had been financial support from Russian interests in the United States. But with the creation of the *Offices russes*, the work of Maklakov and his confrères became financially dependent upon the French Foreign Ministry.

Enjoying many personal acquaintances in the highest reaches of French officialdom and being trusted by the refugees as scrupulously even-handed toward them, Maklakov was a most successful intermediary between the French government and the émigré colony. At the time of his death in 1957, he was still working in the emigration "office" which had long since become wholly a branch of the French administration.

About 50,000 Russian refugees entered France during the twenties on labor contracts made by agents of large industrial and agricultural ministries. There was close cooperation with the International Labor Organization (ILO) (headed by the eminent French socialist, Albert Thomas), which set up hiring centers principally for Russian émigrés in Constantinople, Sofia, Riga, and Warsaw. Contracts guaranteed wages and benefits (such as accident insurance) equal to those earned by the French. But government control of alien workers was very tight. The state determined the worker's wage and place and type of work. He could not change his occupation or residence without authorization. A large majority of contract laborers were single men, and they usually traveled into France together in convoys of ten to twenty. Many knew no French and wore notices around their necks, "Agents of concerned companies are requested to give the bearer all possible aid in reaching the indicated address."[6] Companies frequently constructed dormitories for the single men, varying in size from 50 up to 600 beds. For a modest rent, the men generally got adequate sanitation with hot and cold water baths but their quarters were certainly austere and cramped. The *Société métallurgique de Normandie* built a dorm in Colombelles for a group of bachelor Russian employees. Later, after most of the men had married, the company made over the dorm into family apartments for them.

Men coming in on *métayage* (sharecropping) contracts were subject to especially close supervision. ILO officials screened candidates for suitability and obtained passports and visas for those selected. Groups of about twenty were usually met by French officials in Marseilles or Toulouse and then transferred to their employers. The Agricultural Ministry maintained a service of Russian-speaking inspectors to provide immigrants with advice and guidance for the proper management of their holdings.

Any alien who wished to remain in France for more than two months was obliged to acquire an identity card from the police. Identity cards served as residence permits and were of three types: for non-workers, for workers, and for agricultural laborers. They were normally issued for three years with the possibility of renewal. In 1926, the law established that an alien must have a worker's identity card before taking a job. At that time an émigré could easily obtain such a card, essentially a work permit, from the police providing he was able to produce a contract note from his prospective employer. Until 1934 no restrictions prevented a refugee from working as a craftsman or from opening his own small workshop. But then special "artisan" identity cards were introduced, and their issuance was closely regulated so as to discourage aliens from competing with French artisans.

With the onset of depression, government policy regarding the employment of aliens became increasingly restrictive. Heretofore ambivalent attitudes toward immigration now turned predominantly negative. The political right had favored guest workers to augment the labor force but feared alien threats to national unity and purity. The political left had welcomed refugees in the spirit of internationalism, humanitarianism, and fraternity but suspected that foreign workers took jobs away from Frenchmen and depressed wages. The first indications of economic crisis appeared in France in 1930. The index of industrial production began to fall off, wheat and wine prices declined, and by the end of the year, the iron and coal mining industries were in considerable distress.[7] Organized labor and the nationalist right took alarm and began to demand a government crackdown on immigrant labor.

In 1932 a law was passed authorizing the Labor Ministry to impose quotas for foreign workers in certain areas. Employers or unions had to take the initiative to request a quota, and overall the law had little effect. Russians, though, especially in the Paris area, were hard-hit because of their large numbers in occupations that were effectively restricted. Activist unions obtained quotas for the construction, leather, clothing, millinery, barber, hotel, food and service, and entertainment trades.[8] The most common restriction was 10 percent, but only 5 percent of non-citizens were allowed to be milliners or dressmakers. A good many Russian seamstresses lost their jobs. There were the curious cases of a Russian balalaika orchestra allowed only 15 percent of Russian musicians and a Russian church choir limited to 10 percent of Russian singers.[9] The worst came in 1935. The Labor Ministry refused to issue any new work permits, and those that came up for renewal were delayed for months and then generally cancelled. Even Russian refugees who had been working in France for as long as ten years often lost their work permits. Thousands of Russian émigrés found themselves in desperate straits.

Situations varied with occupation. Those Russians who were engaged in small-scale commerce and industry often suffered from the general effects of the depression, but the government left them alone. Only naturalized citizens were admitted to general medical or dental practice or to the French legal bar association. Several hundred Russian doctors, however, were permitted to practice so long as they treated only Russian patients. They were not qualified to attend persons covered by national health insurance, and as this coverage was expanding in the late thirties, Russian doctors found their opportunities more and more limited. Still, Boris Alexandrovsky survived twenty-one years, studying in university clinics and city hospitals and practicing in dispensaries of "Russian Paris." In 1947, Alexandrovsky was one of 1,500 émigrés who opted for repatriation to the Soviet Union. There he wrote his memoirs, castigating the "bourgeois" French but commiserating with the émigré Russians.[10] Overall, Russians with legal training were better off than physicians or dentists because they were permitted to work as business agents in lower level courts.

Farming opportunities existed even in the years of the depression, especially in the southwest of France. But for people without experience of farm work this was hardly a viable option. Also those refugees who had "workers" permits were usually reluctant to exchange them for agricultural permits, fearing that they probably would not be allowed to change back again.

With the advent of the Popular Front government in 1936, conditions improved somewhat. Inspired by the American New Deal, Premier Léon Blum pledged to employ "the authority of the state ... not to restrict production but to increase consumption ... not to destroy and prohibit, not to ration and limit, but to create and to stimulate ...to breathe life again into an economic organism crushed by the depression and bled by deflation."[11] Committed to combat the rise of fascism in France, Blum's Popular Front government safeguarded civil rights. Labor Minister L. O. Frossard held that the "right to asylum" could not be separated from the "right to work." Refugees whose work permits had been cancelled received new ones. An alien still had to produce a contract note from a willing employer, however, to qualify for a first-time work permit, no easy task in 1936. The restricted percentage rates of aliens allowed in different trades were retained, though now applied less rigorously. The forty-hour work week established by the Popular Front government may have opened up some part-time jobs for non-citizens.

Only 10 percent of French workers were union members before the era of the Popular Front, and few Russian émigrés joined. They were often wary of unions, disliking their leftist orientation or wishing to avoid political involvement which might jeopardize their delicate status. But during the interwar years, some 2,000 émigré taxi drivers did belong to the *Union des chauffeurs russes*. In addition to their typical union concern about wages and working conditions, this group established a Mutual Aid Society through which members could obtain loans (particularly to buy taxis) and legal and medical services. There was a Russian section of the largest French union, the *Confédération générale du travail* (C.G.T.), along with Polish and Italian sections.

Access to social services for the refugees was haphazard. Very much depended on the particular district of residence and the nature of the refugee's occupation. A special group that received French government aid were invalid veterans of the White Army. Their society received an annual donation of Fr. 33,000 (ranging in value from $1,320 to $870) from the government during the 1930s.[12] Customarily, local governments often provided public assistance to émigrés if funds were sufficient. As the refugee population aged, more and more of them fell in need of relief because of illness or accident. Simultaneously, the depression put vastly greater demands upon relief agencies, even as their funds were reduced. Emigrés with a fixed residence were eligible to receive clothing and coupons for such necessities as bread, meat, milk, and coal. They could obtain free medical care in the hospitals and might collect unemployment benefits. But those without a fixed domicile could turn only to private charities.

The Popular Front government moved to extend the range of social services for the entire populace. Old-age pensions, unemployment and sickness benefits, and assistance to the aged, children, pregnant women, nursing mothers, and large families were all to apply to immigrants as well as citizens. But in practice, actual services depended upon local funding. Out of the small number of refugees in Strasbourg in 1938, fifty-one men, forty women, and twenty-seven children– the indigent – did receive government aid. Two widows and three men were receiving assistance, and six unemployed men were collecting benefits. In the Paris district of Billancourt the situation was quite the contrary. About 3,000 Russians resided there in 1938, many formerly employed at the local Renault works. A large number were out of work, and a high percentage were suffering from tuberculosis and heart disease. Some assistance was given, but no unemployment benefits were available in that district. The unemployed consequently tried to move to other areas, such as the Paris fifteenth arrondissement, where unemployment benefits could be obtained.[13]

Administrative practice toward the Russian refugees varied a great deal from one locale to another. In a border town like Strasbourg the threat of expulsion was greater than in the interior. A diplomatic priest or other émigré community spokesman could do much to smooth relations with the authorities. The city of Lyon presented a two-sided picture. On the one hand, some local authorities treated the Russians callously (possibly because of the problems they represented; in the late thirties, unemployment among Russian workers in Lyon was about 45 percent, and many suffered chronic illnesses including tuberculosis). About one hundred of the unemployed had only the Rhône bridges for shelter. French communists in the region tended to be hostile to the refugees as well. On the other hand, relations were quite good between the prefect and mayor and the Lyon Russians. Each year the mayor[14] gave a Christmas tree to the Russian colony and provided a summer vacation camp for them. Marseilles had, after Nice and Lyon, the third largest Russian colony in the provinces. Most lived quietly and respectably, although there was a disreputable element who worked on the docks without permits. The police were aware of this but tolerated it and got on basically well with the Russians. From time to time, a police raid would net several Russians who would be jailed for a short period and then allowed to return to work.[15]

During the depression years, government programs fell far short of providing the relief that many Russian émigrés required. The Russian papers published in Paris regularly carried stories of suicides committed by desperate and starving refugees. The 1933 New Year's Day edition of *The Latest News* carried a story on a thirty-nine-year-old Russian taxi driver in Nice who committed suicide allegedly because of unemployment and starvation. The same paper reported an analogous case almost two years later: "Left without means, the Russian refugee Madame T... threw herself into the Seine with her three-month-old son."[16] Many such examples could be cited. Yet French efforts to provide some relief, especially after the Popular Front reforms of 1936-1937, compared well with other governments of that period.

The naturalization laws of France were similar to those of most European countries. Naturalization was within the discretion of the Justice Ministry. An applicant had to be eighteen years of age, and a continuous residency of at least five years was usually required. (There were interesting exceptions: residency could be cut to one year if, for example, the applicant had served with the French or an allied army, had a French university degree, or was married to a Frenchwoman.) Demonstrated means of financial support, good character, adequate knowledge of the French language, and sponsors' support were all required. Finally, the applicant had to take an oath of allegiance. The wife of an applicant automatically became French upon his naturalization. An émigré Russian woman could similarly achieve instant citizenship by wedding a Frenchman. Minor children were included in a parent's act of naturalization. Either a French father or a French mother conferred French nationality upon their children. Any child born in France was considered a French national (with the right of renunciation upon coming of age), but parents and local authorities were not always aware of this. It sometimes happened that such offspring of Russian refugees were refused benefits like academic scholarships for which French children were eligible. Summing up French naturalization policy, Sir John Hope Simpson observed, "Practice as regards Russian refugees has varied. As a rule, young men who would be liable for military service, agricultural laborers, or families with many children receive favorable consideration. On the other hand, men who are just over thirty years of age, married couples who have no children, and elderly spinsters are not acceptable .... From 1921 to 1934, 17,033 Russian refugees were naturalized in France."[17]

As time went by, increasing numbers of the émigré community became interested in naturalization. It had obvious economic and legal advantages. The earlier attitude that one should remain a "Russian," portrayed by writers like Oldenbourg and Troyat, gradually gave way. In Zoé Oldenbourg's *The Awakened*, Ilya Lanskoi's father does not want his sons to become naturalized French citizens: "Since my sons are considered good enough to be soldiers, I'm not going, hat in hand, to beg for their right to become civil servants."[18] The younger people were more prone to seek citizenship, and this could well cause conflict with older family members. In his novel, *Strangers on Earth* , Henri Troyat shows us this conflict when young Boris decides to apply for French citizenship in 1933. His father and his uncle, an intransigent veteran of the White Army, regard the act as a renunciation, a betrayal of Russia. The stateless Russian, though, was certainly a second-class resident. If he became naturalized, he escaped the quota system imposed on jobs, and he could engage in all trades and most professions. He was free from the threat of expulsion.

One way to attain French citizenship was to serve in the Foreign Legion for three consecutive five-year enlistments. Foreign Legion recruiters signed up Wrangel army veterans in Constantinople, and eventually an estimated 5,000 joined. Most of them stayed with it long enough to achieve French citizenship. Zinovy Peshkov, adopted son of Maxim Gorky, finished his career in the Legion as a brigadier general. Cossacks formed the first Legion cavalry regiment in 1921, and Cossacks and Russians comprised about 35 percent of the Legion's manpower. Legionnaires served in the French colonies, and a few grizzled Russians were still active in Indochina in the early 1950s.[19]

French law provided that resident non-citizens of appropriate sex and age were liable for military service. The refugee colony was very aware of this possibility, and the parents of young men generally contemplated it with foreboding. If their sons were to fight, they thought, let them fight in a Russian "White" army against the Bolsheviks. No refugees were actually called up before 1935. Then they did begin to be called for military training as the threat of Fascism, particularly of Nazi Germany, loomed ever larger.

Native Frenchmen underwent basic training of eighteen months; aliens, six months. Finally, during the very tense summer of 1939, all foreign nationals enjoying asylum in France who were males between the ages of twenty and forty-eight were registered for military service.[20]

Russian émigrés in France generally supported their adopted country on the very eve of the war, although the colony was not innocent of pro-German feelings. Expatriate Russians had commonly sympathized with the Nazi antipathy to Communism, and some had dreamed of joining German forces to destroy the Soviet regime. Then came a diplomatic revolution: Germany and the Soviet Union entered into a mutual non-aggression pact. The world was astonished and Russian refugees perplexed. As they adjusted to this turn of events, the majority of Russians in exile discarded any hopes they may have had in Nazi Germany. Thirty-seven hundred Russians were soldiers in the French army while France was at war with Germany, and the majority of them volunteered.[21]

France attracted refugees because they were better treated there than in most countries. Before the economic crisis, work opportunities in France were relatively good. During the 1930s the threat of expulsion was an extremely grave disability of Russians, and their right to work was limited. Even so, they were better off in France than in many other places. Restrictive regulations were relatively few. The government did not attempt to assimilate children against their parents' wishes. (This often did happen, though, through natural social processes.) Emigré activists were remarkably free in France to form organizations and publish polemics. The exile life in France was a hard one, but the French were generally tolerant, and the government's policy was more often one of benign neglect than of intervention into the émigrés lives.

NOTES TO CHAPTER III

1. D.W. Brogan, *The Development of Modern France, 1870-1939, Vol. II: The Shadow of War, World War I, Between the Wars* , rev. ed. (New York, 1966), 609.

2. Girard and Stoetzel, *Français et immigrés* (Paris: Institut nationale d'etudes démographiques, 1954), 11.

3. "Report on the Work of the High Commissioner for Refugees," *Official Journal* (League of Nations, Sept. 4, 1923), 11.

4. Charles Ledré, *Les émigrés russes en France* (Paris, 1930), 69.

5. Ibid., 70.

6. Georges Mauco, *Les étrangers en France* (Paris, 1932), 127-128.

7. Martin Wolfe, "French Interwar Stagnation Revisited," in *From the Ancien Régime to the Popular Front* , ed. Charles K. Warner (New York, 1969), 164.

8. Gary S. Cross, *Immigrant Workers in Industrial France: The Making of a New Laboring Class* (Philadelphia, 1983), 194.

9. Sir John Hope Simpson, *The Refugee Problem* (London, 1939), 275.

10. Boris N. Alexandrovsky, *Iz perezhitogo v chuzhikh kraiakh, vospominaniia i dumy byvshego emigranta (Experiences in Foreign Climes, Reminiscences and Thoughts of a Former Emigrant* (Moscow, 1969), 66-67.

11. Joel Colton, *Leon Blum, Humanist in Politics* (New York, 1966), 161.

12. Simpson, 184.

13. Ibid., 305, 309.

14. The friendly Lyon mayor was Edouard Herriot, a leader of the Radical Socialist Party and three times premier. Although sympathetic to the exiles, he advocated détente with the Soviet Union and arranged for diplomatic recognition of the Soviet government during his first premiership.

15. Simpson, 306-307.

16. *Posliednaia novosti (Latest News)* , Jan. 1, 1933, 5 and Nov. 15, 1934. The quotation regarding Madame T... and her son is in the Columbia University Bakhmeteff Archive, V.K. Abdank-Kossovskii, Box 1, *Expulsions des réfugiées russes.*

17. Simpson, 599.

18. Zoé Oldenbourg, *The Awakened* (New York, 1957), 96.

19. John A. Hutchins, Jr., "The Wrangel Refugees: A Study of General Baron Peter N. Wrangel's Defeated White Russian Forces, Both Military and Civilian, in Exile," unpubl. MA thesis (University of Louisville, 1972), 145-147.

20. Jacques Vernant, *The Refugee in the Post-War World* (New Haven, 1953), 265.

21. Louis Chevalier et al., *Documents sur l'immigration*, travaux et documents, cahier no. 2 (Paris Institut nationale d'études démographiques, 1947), 148-149.

IV. United States Government and the Refugees

Give me your tired, your poor,
Your huddled masses yearning to breathe free,
The wretched refuse of your teeming shore,
Send these, the homeless, tempest-tossed to me:
I lift my lamp beside the golden door.

Thus did New York City-born Emma Lazarus express the ideal of the United States as a land of refuge, of political asylum. "Mother of Exiles" she called the Statue of Liberty, that paramount symbol of political liberty, created for the Americans by their oldest ally, the French. The statue was a gift to commemorate the centennial of American independence. When she took her place in New York Harbor in 1886, the most massive inpouring of immigrants that the United States would ever experience was gathering volume. This was the so-called "new immigration" stemming largely from southern and eastern Europe. Over 1,000,000 people were entering the United States annually on the eve of the First World War. The largest influx ever from the Russian Empire arrived in 1913. They were predominantly Jews, included Poles and other ethnic groups as well as Russians, and their total number was 291,040.[1] Jews were almost always true refugees, fleeing religious persecution and occasional murderous pogroms in Russia. The great majority of newcomers, though, were not seeking asylum, but economic opportunity. Had they come as victims, they might have been received with more compassion.

This massive wave of "new immigration" churned up popular alarm at foreign inundation, and from the 1880s many Americans began to think of their land less as a place of refuge and more as a beleaguered bastion. The throngs of incoming Italians and Slavs raised fears that the Anglo-Saxon foundations of the nation would be undermined. Horrified nativists imagined that mentally inferior races were polluting native stock and augmenting criminal and even lunatic behavior. Alarmists interpreted the results of First World War army mental tests (designed and administered with amazing ineptitude) as proving the defective intelligence of the Italian and Slavic "races." These unsound minds (often in unsound bodies, it was believed) embraced highly suspect religious beliefs including Catholicism, Eastern Orthodoxy, and Judaism. Such outlandish and exotic convictions would surely never merge into the bedrock of native Protestantism, the quintessentially "American" faith stemming from the Puritan Fathers.

Political and economic objections to immigration supplemented the

32

racist and religious ones. The newcomers were said to be hostile to democratic institutions, fomenters of anarchy and socialism, opponents of private property and free speech. They would not unite with the body
politic, but would remain enclaves apart, sustaining themselves through
their 1,500 foreign language newspapers. "Why try to make Americans
out of those who will always be Americanski?" impatiently asked *The
Saturday Evening Post.*[2] Unions opposed immigration, claiming that aliens
glutted the labor force and depressed wages. The unemployment and
housing shortage following World War I reinforced this fear of immigrants as competitors for limited jobs and resources. American economic
expansion from 1922 to 1929 eased such concern, but then the years of the
Great Depression dramatically resurrected it.

About 20,000 Russians who were refugees from the revolution entered
the United States between the world wars; some 6,000 settled in New
York City.[3] These were only one-tenth of the number to be found in
France and in Paris, an indication of France's importance as a stronghold
of the White emigration. U.S. law, unlike that of most European states
including France, made no distinction between an "immigrant" and a
"refugee." In practice, American authorities relaxed the usual standards
when granting entry visas to bona fide refugees. A refugee's lack of documents might be overlooked, and he or she not be subjected to the litera-
cy test which had been required of immigrants since 1917. (They had to
demonstrate the ability to read a language of their choice.) But once
applicants gained entry to the United States, they all shared a common
status defined by immigration law. By the time any significant number of
Whites began to arrive in the States, there was no special authority to
look after their interests.

When the Bolsheviks seized power in November 1917, Boris
Bakhmeteff was the Russian Ambassador to the United States. A busi-
nessman and engineer, he had been sent as the head of an extraordinary
mission, charged to obtain all possible American aid in prosecuting the
war effort. The Bolsheviks, of course, had long been inveighing against
Russia's commitment to fight and against the Provisional Government
which had appointed Bakhmeteff. The Soviet regime quickly disavowed
all incumbent ambassadors; nonetheless, the U.S. government continued
to accord Bakhmeteff full diplomatic status until he chose to step down in
June 1922. He in no way represented the Soviet Union, but American
authorities persistently regarded the Communist government as a temporary aberration. Meanwhile Bakhmeteff was allowed to dispose of
Russian credits in the United States, and he expended over $77,000,000.
Much of the money was used to help support the political activities of the
White refugee organizations centered in Paris and to aid the White armies
and the great mass of exiles who evacuated the Crimea with Wrangel.
When Bakhmeteff retired in 1922, there was no offical figure in the United
States to speak for White émigrés, no one like Vasily Maklakov in France.[4]

Those Russian exiles who entered the United States in the early twenties had to deal with an overall immigration policy that did not take their particular situation into account. Popular and often incoherent fears of immigrants were reflected in two complementary types of federal policy. First, the federal government attempted to control aliens already within the county. Second, the government by stages implemented a restrictive quota system of immigration. The threat of government repression and clear-cut entry restriction met all immigrants coming into the United States after the World War.

The Industrial Workers of the World was one of the first organizations to trigger repressive government measures. Public fears of alien influences during the First World War were frequently inflamed by the IWW, perceived as foreign-dominanted, radical, and disloyal. Many alien, immigrant workers were members of the IWW which was a revolutionary, syndicalist trade union. But the union had been founded in Chicago in 1905 by such well-known American labor leaders as William D. (Big Bill) Haywood, Vincent St. John, and the omnipresent "Mother" Mary Jones. Haywood and St.John were leaders of the militant Western Federation of Miners. Mother Jones was a fierce advocate of labor rights, and over a fifty-year period she seemed to appear at every major management-labor confrontation, urging on the strikers. The IWW grew out of the violent struggle between segments of American industry and labor, a ferocious conflict in which miners and loggers were prominent. When the war ended, a number of states successfully prosecuted IWW members under new criminal syndicalism laws. These laws sanctioned conviction for mere membership in suspect organizations or espousal of unpopular views. Under federal law such charges could not be brought, but aliens were subject to deportation without trial. In 1919, more than 3,000 aliens were deported from the United States, for causes ranging from indigence to suspected anarchy.[5] An immigrant was subject to deportation until he became naturalized, and that power was the federal government's most potent control over resident non-citizens.

Attorney General A. Mitchell Palmer, "the fighting Quaker," would use the weapon of deportation most dramatically against the Red Menace. Palmer launched a series of raids against suspected subversives, abetted by his special assistant, J. Edgar Hoover. A special Bureau of Investigation was set up under Hoover to carry out this work, prototype of the FBI which was instituted in 1924 with Hoover as director. Hundreds of members of the Union of Russian Workers were taken into custody in November and December of 1919. Among them were the much publicized anarchists, Emma Goldman and Alexander Berkman. Berkman was Polish, but most of those arrested were Russian in origin. In extremely short order, 249 of those who had been seized were bound for the Soviet Union. On 21 December 1919, the Army Transport Ship Buford sailed from Ellis Island. Fourteen of the deportees were non-politicals, nine of them, "likely to become a public charge." The rest were accused of advocating the overthrow of the government. They docked at Hango, Finland, on 16 January 1920, and three days later crossed into the U.S.S.R. by train.[6] The sailing of the Buford (dubbed the "Red Arc") received extensive press coverage, particularly because the infamous Goldman and Berkman were aboard.

The first week of January 1920 saw the dragnet thrown over two largely immigrant organizations, the Communist Party of America and Communist Labor Party. Raids carried out across the country were so carelessly executed that among the thousands arrested were a good many non-party members and even citizens, including war veterans. An appalled immigration commissioner in Seattle described the chaos: "The police, acting upon instructions of the Department of Justice, went into the restaurants, pool rooms, lodging houses, cigar stores, and the different places downtown, and rounded up everyone in those different places, regardless of whether a man was eating his dinner or not, and brought them to the station." The commissioner, Henry M. White, went on to describe how 350 men were arrested and how inspectors worked through the night questioning them and ended by releasing all but twenty-seven the following day.[7]

Palmer's Justice Department instigated the raids, but authority to deport radical aliens was reserved to the Secretary of Labor by the wartime Sedition Act. The Labor Department, jealous of its prerogative in the treatment of immigrants, ruled that mere membership in a Communist party was not ground for deportation. Louis F. Post, the Assistant Secretary of Labor, was particularly zealous in curbing the strong-arm tactics used by agents of the Justice Department and the Bureau of Investigation. Ultimately he endorsed the deportation of only 556 out of the 3,000 detainees arrested in January raids.[8] Very few true Russian revolutionaries intended to stir up trouble in the U.S.A. (Emma Goldman might be considered an exception, but she had come to the States when seventeen and had been a resident for thirty-three years. She was a self-proclaimed anarchist, appalled by her experiences in the U.S.S.R. After Goldman and Berkman got out, her scathing indictment of Bolshevik tyranny, *My Disillusionment in Russia* was published in 1922.) The typical alien Russian radical avidly followed events in the Soviet Union, and thousands voluntarily returned there to participate in the revolutionary experiment. But most of the 556 forcibly deported were indeed Russians, and the accompanying uproar was a grave blow to the entire immigrant Russian community.

In the glaring publicity of the Palmer raids, public opinion tainted all Russian-American (commonly thought of as Jews), citizens and non-citizens, as potentially disloyal radicals. Even the conservative Russian Mutual Aid Society in America (ROOVA) recalled these events years later with deep dismay. In its 1936 jubilee report, the Society referred to the "over 10,000 Russian immigrants" arrested (an exaggeration). "All radi-

cal papers and journals were raided and their employees arrested. All
cultural life of the Russian colony was paralyzed. But it has successfully
revived."[9] The officers of ROOVA in 1936 were anti-Soviet, and they were
not likely to have been radical at the time of the Palmer raids, but
nonetheless, they perceived that time as a very dark one for the Russian
community as a whole. Something of that atmosphere accosted the
Russian refugees who arrived in considerable numbers in 1921 to 1927,
helping to sustain fears of foreigners, "damned radicals and anarchists."

The Immigration Quota Act of 1921 expressed Congress's opposition
to alien intrusion. Quotas were based on "national origins" and it was
birthplace, not citizenship or recent residence, that counted. So the
Russian quota applied to all persons born within the territory of the
Soviet Union — excepting Asians. Various formulas were applied which
limited the annual immigration of those born on Russian or Soviet soil to
between 2,000 and 3,000. In the 1920s, the major justification for restrict-
ing immigration was to encourage racial homogeneity. Northern and
western Europeans comprised 82 percent of all authorized immigrants.
Southern and eastern Europeans including the Russians were limited to
16 percent. Asians were entirely excluded. Following the 1929 economic
collapse, restrictionists emphasized the need to preserve "American jobs
for Americans." Any applicant "likely to become a public charge" could
be refused, and throughout the depression years only the most prosperous were admitted. Quotas ceased to be filled; the numbers of Russians
entering in the decade of the 1930s were only 20 to 25 percent of what
they had been in the 1920s, a pattern typical of all national groups.

Visa applicants who had immediate family members in the United
States received preference but were still subject to the quota. This was a
source of the greatest anxiety to U.S. immigrants. In 1924, six émigré
organizations representing 5,000 Russians in the San Francisco area petitioned President Coolidge. They asked for his support of an amendment
to the immigration law "that would admit outside the quota all members
of the immediate families of aliens now in this county."[10] Such an amendment had no chance, however, given the powerful restrictionist senti-
ment in Congress.

Both the Justice and Labor Departments were involved in deportation
proceedings, and three federal departments, State, Treasury, and Labor,
jointly administered the immigration quota law. State Department con-
suls abroad processed visa applications and decided who would receive
the limited number of immigration visas. A Public Health Surgeon, who
was a Treasury Department officer, had to certify the applicant's physical
and mental fitness. Immigration officials who double-checked credentials
at ports of entry were Labor Department employees. Initially an applicant was required to furnish the consul with "two copies of his 'dossier'
and prison and military record, two certified copies of his birth certificate, and two copies of all other available public records concerning him
kept by the Government to which he owes allegiance."[11] These require-

ments could be waived by a consul in the case of a bona fide refugee.

All aliens in the United States faced work restrictions. U.S. law strictly forbade contract labor, so no immigrants were permitted to enter into employment agreements before they arrived in America. This was the opposite of French practice whereby the government actively supported foreign labor contracting. State laws closed off certain occupations to aliens. Commonly citizenship was a prerequisite for government service itself. Many professions and trades requiring licensing or certification were closed to non-citizens. Doctors and lawyers were generally shut out, although the émigré Society of Russian Physicians was able to have some of its members admitted to practice by 1925. Ninety to ninety-five percent of the Russian refugees entering the United States found their first jobs as unskilled laborers. Some unions were open to them, some were not.

Job discrimination against non-citizens was especially severe during the depression, and this pressured larger numbers to apply for naturalization. Many refugees had resisted giving up their Russian citizenship, thinking it a betrayal of the Motherland, pre-Soviet Russia, which they hoped would be restored. Thirty-six hundred applicants for citizenship (ethnicity not specified) were polled in 1932 as to their motivations, and 29 percent stated that their aim was to hold or get jobs. In the words of Harold Fields, "as an alien he is ineligible on the average to three out of every five jobs and to four out of every five labor-union memberships; innumerable laws shut the door to occupations and professions that he may be seeking to enter."[12]

The federal government's active support of the union movement during the depression years did encourage increasing union activity on the part of Russian immigrants. The largest number of Russians were members of the United Mine Workers and the Steel Worker's Union, although most of these had settled in the United States before the revolution. Many Jewish Russian émigrés found a place in Sidney Hillman's Amalgamated Clothing Workers of America. There was a Russian-language monthly bulletin put out by this union which especially addressed the concerns of tailors. Russian-language newspapers not infrequently appealed to readers for donations to strike funds; e.g., in April 1928, a Pittsburgh group called for additional money to help support striking coal-miners. They had so far collected $360.[13] Russian-Americans were a majority in the Stone Masons, Window-Washers, and Housewreckers' Unions in New York City. Earlier immigrants had established Russian branches of some unions where a few newcomers in the twenties could find a niche, e.g., Russian Branch of Clockmakers; Russian Branch of Garment Workers; Society of Russian Bootmakers; Society of Russian Mechanics; New York Union of Russian Dockworkers. White émigrés who were union members were unlikely to be militants in the American labor struggles. Those who were politically active tended to focus on Soviet rather than

American issues. The typical White, of course, was vehemently anti-Soviet whether politically active or not.

During the war the federal government had set up the Foreign Language Governmental Information Bureau to disseminate information primarily about American war policy to foreign language residents of the United States. When the war ended, the bureau became affiliated with the Red Cross, and it continued to be a significant source of public affairs information in a variety of languages. In the twenties and thirties the Foreign Language Information Service, as it was then called, served the Russian community in a number of ways. It sent news releases to the Russian press in the United States, provided Russian translations of various items and sponsored Russian language lectures on American culture. Russian community affairs were covered as well as public affairs in general, and the Service offered useful advice on such things as the immigration quota law. The Service also regularly published news releases in English, sympathetically interpreting the plight of immigrants to native Americans.

Once it issued a permanent residence visa to a newcomer, the government took no direct action to promote naturalization. There were private groups that encouraged "Americanization" and naturalization, and generally immigrants felt more inducement to naturalize in the United States than elsewhere. The prominent journalist and editor, Mark Vishniak, remarked on this after he arrived in the States in 1940, having fled the Nazi occupation of France. Vishniak noted that whereas the French extended citizenship selectively and for particular services or because of special connections in France, the Americans encouraged naturalization for all. He asserted this even though the FBI suspected him of being a Marxist. Vishniak had belonged to the Socialist Revolutionary Party in Russia, a populist movement chiefly concerned with peasant problems. He was never an orthodox Marxist and never supported the Bolsheviks. Despite the Bureau's suspicions, Vishniak attained citizenship after eight years in the United States.[14]

A sole federal agency, the Bureau of Naturalization, used its resources indirectly to facilitate citizenship training. The Bureau was in regular communication with boards of education and interested associations to promote classes for aliens in English and citizenship. It furnished free materials such as the Federal Citizenship Textbook, Naturalization Information Forms, and posters and guidelines for conducting classes. Industrial concerns sometimes used these Bureau aids to establish classes for their immigrant workers. In prewar Ford Motor Company classes, the first phrase that immigrants had been taught to repeat was "I am an American."[15]

Until 1921, most state governments and boards of education were active in sponsoring Americanization programs, usually by appropriating funds for teaching English in evening schools. "The school year 1919 closed with 2,240 communities actively supporting the movement and carrying on classes on behalf of the immigrant."[16] The new quota law soon made its impact, though, and the numbers enrolled in these classes considerably dwindled. When the Bureau raised its naturalization fee from $5 to $20 in 1929, the result was a sharp decline in applications.[17] Modest immigrant educational programs barely stayed alive through the depression years. The Adult Education Program of the Works Progress Administration (WPA) gave some support to courses in English and in Americanization. The Americanization movement was tainted at its height in 1919 to 1921 by Red-baiting and self-righteous chauvinism, but in the long run it helped establish the concept of adult education and it stimulated academic study of the immigration phenomenon.

Applicants for U.S. citizenship were in the charge of the Bureau of Naturalization, under the Secretary of Labor. As in France, any child born in the country automatically became a citizen. And minor children were included when their parents naturalized. Children of an American father were deemed American. But an American woman married to a foreigner acquired her husband's nationality, as did their children. An alien woman who married an American had to apply for citizenship and to satisfy the major requirements if she wished to be naturalized.

An immigrant wishing to naturalize could apply for his declaration of intent, "the first papers," anytime after his arrival. He could apply for his final citizenship certificate, "second papers," after a minimum five-year residence in the country. Two witnesses, U.S. citizens, had to testify on behalf of the petitioner, affirming his good moral character. The new citizen had to be at least eighteen years of age, speak English, swear to support the principles of the U.S. Constitution, and renounce allegiance to his native land. This last requirement was initially a sticking point for many of the White émigrés. They could easily renounce the Soviet regime, but not their "native land." In striking contrast to their fellow exiles in France, though, almost all the émigrés in the United States were naturalized before the Second World War. Two of the largest Russian refugee groups in America were surveyed in 1938. Ninety percent of them had become American citizens, out of 2,500 in Seattle and 6,000 in New York City.[18] U.S. immigrants were officially and popularly encouraged to naturalize; French immigrants were not; and that helps to explain the much higher percentage of naturalized Whites in the U.S.A. than in France.

Although U.S. law held aliens liable for military service under the same conditions as citizens, there was no draft between the two world wars, so the question of military service was not an issue for immigrants in the United States as it was in France. Almost alone among governments, the United States did not require aliens to register. That changed in 1940 with adoption of the Alien Registration Act which has since mandated the registration and fingerprinting of resident foreigners. But the former absence of any such obligation helped to create that relatively free atmosphere which immigrants noted in the United States.

Some, but not all, social benefits were extended to aliens on an equal basis with citizens. Federal work relief during the depression was available only to those aliens who had taken out first naturalization papers. Social security and unemployment benefits that came in with the New Deal were extended to all U.S. residents, regardless of citizenship. At first the WPA made no distinctions, but in 1937 it dismissed non-citizens from its employ. Many Russian musicians, painters, and sculptors who had become naturalized, though, continued to participate actively in WPA concerts and in the decoration of public buildings. State pension laws generally did not apply to aliens, whereas state relief laws were "on the whole ... fair to the immigrant." That was so partly because "the percentage of non-citizens on relief has been found to be small throughout the country."[19] The United States government had a fair record of extending benefits to alien refugees. For both citizens and non citizens alike, however, relief was more likely to come from private organizations in the United States than in European countries. The French state, for one, was more predisposed to assume social service functions than the American government.

Official U.S. treatment of refugees compared well with the policies of other governments in terms of humanity and fairness. Once émigrés got to the United States, they were delighted not to have to register with the police or to carry identity cards. The immigration quota system imposed in 1921 was, it is true, a great barrier to be overcome. The era of the United States as an open land of asylum was ended, and the numbers of Russian refugees admitted were considerably fewer than those desirous of entry. The "Red Scare" of the early twenties created a frightening climate for immigrants, generally stirring up currents of intolerant nativism. Repression tended to fall on earlier Russian immigrants, though, rather than on those who fled the 1917 revolution and subsequent civil war. To an even greater extent than in France, the typical Russian émigré (after the Palmer raids had passed) in the United States was left alone. He had no special status as "refugee" and could consequently live more like an ordinary native American. He certainly found an atmosphere more conducive to naturalization in the States than in European countries like France.

NOTES TO CHAPTER IV

1. Hannibal G. Duncan, *Immigration and Assimilation* (Boston, 1933), 274.

2. *Saturday Evening Post*, 193 (May 14, 1921): 20, cited in John Higham, *Strangers in the Land: Patterns of American Nativism, 1860-1925*, 2nd ed. (New Brunswick, NJ, 1963), 262.

3. Sir John Hope Simpson, *The Refugee Problem* (London, 1939), 468-469.

4. Frederick Lewis Schuman, *American Policy Toward Russia since 1917* (New York), 224-228. Bakhmeteff became a Columbia University professor and began collecting material on the White emigration that is the nucleus of the Columbia University Bakhmeteff Archive.

5. Deportation statistics cited in William Preston, Jr., *Aliens and Dissenters: Federal Suppression of Radicals. 1903-1933* (Cambridge, MA, 1963), 334.

6. Report from Supervising Immigrant Inspector, F.W. Berkshire, to Commissioner General of Immigration, Feb. 11, 1920 (54235/36G, Russian Radicals, 1919-20), Subject Correspondence, 1906-1932, INS *Central Office*, RG 85, National Archives of the United States.

7. "Letter from Henry M. White, Commissioner in Seattle, to Commissioner General of Immigration, " Jan. 26, 1920 (37012, General), Subject Correspondence, 1906-1932, INS *Central Office*, RG 85, National Archives.

8. Higham, 230-231.

9. *Desiat' let zhizni ROOVA, 1926-1936 (Ten Years in the Life of ROOVA)* (New York, 1936), 141.

10. "Among the Foreign Born," *The Interpreter*, 4 (Jan. 1925): 14.

11. Immigration Act of 1924. Sec. 7 (c), cited by Simpson, 610.

12. Harold Fields, "Why Aliens Seek Citizenship," *Commonweal*, 16 (June 15, 1932), 181. Harold Fields was executive director of the National League for American Citizenship, a refreshingly enlightened Americanization organization.

13. *Novoe russkoe slovo (New Russian Word)* (April 6, 1928), 3. This is the oldest Russian-American newspaper still being published. It was founded in 1910.

14. Mark Vishniak, *Years of Emigration, 1919-1969, Paris-New York* (Stanford, CA, 1970), 215 (in Russian).

15. Leonard Dinnerstein et al., *Natives and Strangers: Ethnic Groups and the Building of America* (New York), 184.

16. Edward George Hartmann, *The Movement to Americanize the Immigrant* (New York, 1948), 235.

17. "Introduction" (E-1—E-30-1029), Dist. 3 (NY), Citizenship Education File, Records of the Immigration and Naturalization Service, RG 85, National Archives.

18. Simpson, 469-470.

19. Harold Fields, *The Refugee in the United States* (New York, 1938), 49-50.

V. "Little Russias" in Paris and New York

EMIGRES IN PARIS

The Orthodox Church

As escaped refugees clustered in their far-flung exile communities, they typically established Russian Orthodox churches as the anchor points in their new havens. The church provided vital spiritual sustenance for those who had lost so much, and it also served as a social and commercial center. In the words of the émigré journalist, Parchevsky, "The Russian Church is the emigration center for preservation and passing on of Russian culture. Around it group a Russian library, school, theater, club. It again takes up its medieval role — the provider of enlightenment."[1] Stalls would appear in the churchyard, vendors offering samples of Russian fare, blintzes, sausage, pickled cucumbers, and smoked herring. The churchyard was the favorite meeting place. After services émigrés would gather there, sometimes by the hundreds, and it was not uncommon for long-lost acquaintances to discover one another on such occasions. The enveloping babble of Russian language made the participants feel at home as they exchanged letters, stories, and memories. Shops and restaurants catering to the Russians were often to be found close by the church, convenient sites for notice boards with employment information and queries and announcements of all kinds.

A few Russian churches had been built in Europe to serve members of the diplomatic corps and tourists. One of the most elaborate was the Byzantine-style St. Alexander Nevsky Cathedral on the rue Daru in Paris. It was constructed during the 1850s thanks in part to a personal donation of 200,000 francs by Tsar Alexander II. Now this magnificent building with its gilt, onion-shaped domes, crenelated stoneworks, icons, and frescoes, became the headquarters of the church in exile. When the first refugees arrived in Paris, the only Russian church was the rue Daru cathedral, but more than thirty others were erected during the following decade.

The new churches built by émigrés were usually in working class neighborhoods and quite modest. One Parisian shelter for Russian refugees converted a garage in its courtyard into an Orthodox chapel. A large neighboring garage belonged to a communist union (*syndicat*), but its employees were quite willing to help out the Russians and aided them in constructing the chapel.[2] Particularly heroic conversions were made in Grenoble, where a cave was turned into a chapel, and in Annecy, where part of an abandoned and dilapidated prison was transformed. Both of these efforts were acclaimed for their beautiful decoration. In Paris some workers contracted with their employers to withhold two percent of their wages, for the church and priest. But there was a severe shortage of clergy, and in quite a few parishes a priest would officiate only on rare occasions. In the territory of Western Europe under the jurisdiction of Metropolitan Eulogy were over 100 parishes. Almost all of them maintained charities, mutual aid and burial funds, libraries, and schools.

The Russian Orthodox Church derives from the Byzantine rite, and its bishops and "metropolitans" (equivalent to archbishops) traditionally recognized a Moscow patriarch as the head of the church. That was until Peter the Great ended the elections of patriarchs, he and his successors preferring to dominate the church through the Holy Synod which they controlled. But even as the Bolsheviks were seizing power in November 1917, church dignitaries elected Metropolitan Tikhon to be the first Moscow patriarch in 217 years. Tikhon was to undergo stormy relations with the Soviet government, including a period of imprisonment, but he found a modus vivendi with the new regime by agreeing to remove the church entirely from politics.

Tikhon raised Eulogy to the rank of metropolitan and named him head of the Russian churches in western Europe. Meanwhile, in 1921, a council of émigré clergy met in Yuglosavia and denounced the Soviet regime in resounding terms. They prayed that God might "return to the All-Russian Throne the Anointed, a lawful Orthodox Tsar of the House of Romanov."[3] Tikhon felt compelled to disavow the Yugoslav council, and its supporters have since maintained their own separate ecclesiastical jurisdiction, "The Orthodox Synod (now Church) Abroad." This reactionary group established their own church in Paris on the rue d'Odessa, challenging Eulogy's authority. The cathedral of rue Daru retained by far the larger membership, but the grand-ducal families and many prominent nobles preferred the rue d'Odessa church.

After 1930 Eulogy too broke with Moscow and submitted to the Istanbul patriarch, his jurisdiction being known as the West-European Eparchy. The Church Abroad and the Eparchy remain separate to this day, and in addition there were a few churches outside the U.S.S.R. directly subordinate to the Moscow patriarch, so there is a three-way split. These jurisdictional disputes caused no little consternation among the émigrés. Many had gratefully regarded the church as the sole institution that could bind them together irrespective of their political differences. Such was not the case.

In spite of these political dissensions, the majority of the émigré clergy were anxious to avoid overt partisanship. In the rue Daru cathedral, for example, masses for the dead omitted any references to the titles of the murdered royal family. Thus a good number of intellectuals, who had detested the church before the revolution as hopelessly reactionary, now became regular attendees. The orthodox service, the magnificent choral music, the incense, the icons in flickering candlelight created an atmosphere reminiscent of "home." On the other hand, where the community was not so cohesive or the church so impressive, attendance gradually diminished. The lack of suitable clothing, the need to work, the example of non-practicing French Catholics, the absence of constraints, the depth of despair, all could lead to an ultimate separation from the church.[4]

The Emigré Press

Many professional writers and journalists left Russia with the White emigration, and in exile they published extensively. About 1,500 Russian-language periodicals and thousands of books were printed worldwide during the twenties and thirties. Prague and Paris became the émigré publishing centers. Altogether, more than 100 Russian language publishers were active in Europe, America and Asia.

The YMCA Press, for example, has been a long-time publisher of important Russian works in literature, religious thought and philosophy. The YMCA began this effort as a service to Russian prisoners-of-war in Austrian camps. It functioned in Berlin for several years and then permanently located in Paris in 1925. Between the wars the press used one of the ten Russian printing shops of Paris and issued many practical textbooks as well as religious and philosophical studies. There were fourteen Russian-language bookstores in Paris that dealt in new and used books and stocked both Soviet and émigré publications. The refugees in Paris enjoyed a diversity and freedom of their own written language such as had never existed and is yet to exist in their homeland.

Periodicals ran the gamut from the specialized to the general. Newsletters and reports were put out by political factions, professional, veteran, student and religious groups, charities, and academic and cultural associations. The Russian tradition of publishing "thick magazines" was carried on by *Contemporary Annals (Sovremennye zapiski)*. Those "thick magazines" had appealed to the broad reading public with a combination of belles lettres and literary and political commentary of considerable lengthiness and detail. *Contemporary Annals*, published in Paris from 1920 to 1940, maintained this tradition at the highest standard and published articles across the cultural and artistic spectrum by all the outstanding émigré writers. Emigrés also established some journals in French for the edification of their hosts. Two notable anti-Soviet reviews were *Russie opprimée* and *Cause commune*. The weekly or bi-weekly *Russia*

Illustrated (Illustrirovannaia Rossiia) appealed to a wide spectrum of readers in the Paris Russian colony. This popular photo-journal reported mainly on events inside the Soviet Union and on exile life in Paris. Following a Russian newspaper tradition, it also published fiction. The first issue in 1924 featured stories by the prominent authors Bunin and Kuprin and a poem of Bal'mont's. There were straightforward reports of official pronouncements in the U.S.S.R. and also exposés with photos of poor students, homeless children, beggars, etc. The August 4, 1928, issue ran a photo of Fridtjof Nansen meeting with Soviet planners of a dirigible expedition over the Arctic. The caption read "Emigrant Commissar — Friend of the Soviets." The editors ironically commented that Nansen was more competent in arctic exploration than in refugee affairs. No friend of the Soviets could be a friend to Russian refugees.

Russia Illustrated's theater and arts section highlighted Russian performers. There were a children's page and a women's page. The paper ran many human interest stories about the émigrés in Paris, and it carried appeals to aid the needy. A mail box section included requests for correspondence, for information, for potential marriage partners, and for missing persons. Beauty contests were promoted by the newspapers; for instance, *Russia Illustrated* sponsored "Miss Russia" in 1931. Each year Miss Russia entered the Miss Europe and Miss Universe contests; consequently, those competitions represented one of the few areas of interaction between the émigré community and society at large. The advertisements revealed a good deal about exile life: broker Matusovsky offered émigrés fair prices for valuables. Restaurants, schools, shops, clothing stores, pharmacies, banks, real estate agencies, hotels, even a construction company, catered to Russians. To serve them were butchers, fortune-tellers, mechanics, and French and English teachers. One could buy Russian Sappho cigarettes. The Russian Albatross Film Company produced movies directed and acted entirely by émigrés. A celebrated example of émigré film work, recently restored, is Alexander Volkoff's *Casanova,* starring Ivan Mosjoukine.

Two daily papers competed for the Russian reading audience in Paris and, indeed, through the diaspora. The one with the most extensive coverage of the Soviet Union and with the largest circulation, 30,000 to 35,000, was *Latest News (Poslednie novosti).* This paper, "to the left" in the view of most émigrés, was edited by Pavel Miliukov, eminent historian and leader of the Constitutional Democratic Party during the years of tsarism. An Anglophile and staunch defender of traditional Russian diplomatic interests, Miliukov had served briefly as foreign minister under the Provisional Government. Although firmly anticommunist and anti-soviet, Miliukov's years as a harsh critic of authoritarian tsarism and advocate of a democratic-parliamentary regime placed him in the left wing of émigré political opinion. But *Latest News* was respected for its high journalistic standards and unparalleled coverage of Soviet develop-

ments, which a great many refugees avidly followed. Each day the Soviet
government bought several hundred copies of this paper, to monitor
émigré thinking and discover how much information about Soviet affairs
was leaking out.

The more conservative daily, *Renaissance (Vozrozhdenie)*, ˛ as the
major competing paper. It too had an extensive and widespread
readership. *Renaissance* allotted considerable space to literary and artistic
reviews, featuring such well-known writers as Kuprin, Zaitsev, and
Merezhkovsky. It was militantly anti-communist and among its writers
were monarchists, but like all the major periodicals, it avoided the dog-
matic and the extreme in order to appeal to the widest possible circle of
readers. Poet Marina Tsvetaeva struck the right note with her 1926 New
Year's wish: "For Russia – a Bonaparte, for myself – publishers."
Renaissance carried a lot of news about the Soviet Union, including
excerpts reprinted from Soviet magazines and journals. Much space was
given over to appeals for charity and reports on the progress of various
fund-raising drives, all to benefit the Russian colony. The editors were
imbued with a spirit of community service, exemplified by an article published as Europe plunged into war in September 1939. The possibility of
evacuating Paris was discussed with instructions for putting documents
in order in time of peril. Readers also received information about air raid
warnings and issuance of gas masks.[5]

The two dailies regularly published names of missing persons, asking
readers to send in any information regarding their whereabouts. There
were rundowns about émigrés in various countries. *Latest News* carried
an "Information Section" in which it listed the addresses and open hours
of Russian-oriented institutions: the Russian Embassy and Consulate in
Paris; the Turgenev Library; a Russian officers' dormitory and cafeteria;
the church on rue Daru. Schedules were printed for Russian organization
meetings, lectures, church services, balls, and holiday celebrations. The
paper instituted a free help-wanted and jobs-sought service. A
"Questions and Answers" column gave practical advice on changing
jobs, acquiring documents, legalities, useful addresses, etc. *Latest News*
like its rival reported on the literary and artistic scene, plays, films, and
radio programs, and it published serialized stories which were sometimes translations. During the difficult economic year of 1933, *Latest News*
invited readers to its offices daily at 6:00 p.m. for free advice concerning
identity cards, visas, and job-hunting. Donors and the amounts of their
gifts to Russian charitable organizations were listed.

Advertisements and notices in the two dailies portray the Russian
colony as a little world in itself complete. Consumers could choose
among Russian grocery, clothing, furniture, book, and liquor stores. For
the often impecunious readers there was "Great choice of used men's
suits from the best Paris tailors — five percent discount to disabled veterans.... Sale of over 100 worn gowns from fine dressmakers — 150 francs

and up."[6] One could frequent a Russian fortune teller, tailor or furrier, antique dealer, jeweler, photographer, book publisher, typesetter, or printer. Legal aid, translation services, and a Russian labor exchange were available. Russian physicians, dentists, clinics, and pharmacies offered health services. Several hotels catered to a Russian clientele. Those able to afford domestic service could find Russian cooks, seam-stresses, governesses, and companions for the elderly. One could master a trade through Russian correspondence school, take music and singing lessons, learn French or English, and gain expertise in the art of Swedish massage. Winnings in a Russian lottery might be spent on Russian the-ater or sport, orchestra or dance band, restaurant or café. Russian real estate agencies included listings of summer houses. Russian banks and export and import services promised to keep the émigrés' finances in order.

There was within the emigration, most notably in Paris, a remarkable tendency for organized activity to fall into "left" and "right" factions. Paralleling the ideological split between *Latest News* and *Renaissance* were two academic societies, two and even three church jurisdictions, two pro-fessional organizations of engineers, of lawyers, of ex-marines. By the 1930s the significance of these divisions often became blurred. To call this one a "leftist" could mean that he read the Soviet press; to call that one a "rightist" could mean that he found fault with *Latest News*. But older émi-grés continued to be aware of their former political convictions.[7] The two great dailies reflected, however nebulously, this fundamental division.

In 1923 regular postal service to the U.S.S.R. was established, and a considerable business of sending food parcels to friends and relatives developed, with ads frequently appearing in the newspapers. In 1932, for example, one could send a standard package containing 100 grams of tea, 400 grams of coffee, 2,000 grams of rice, 1,000 grams of grits, and 1,000 grams of tapioca. The cost was seventy francs plus about thirty-five francs in duty ($4.20).[8]

A Russian almanac published in Paris in 1931 carried a wealth of useful information for the émigrés. It listed the religious holidays including Muslim ones, and also featured an agricultural calendar. There was infor-mation on good farm land available in France, the French Riviera, climat-ic zones, health services, first-aid measures, Russian publications, Russian workers and invalid veterans in France, legal services, owning and operating an automobile, building a home on the installment plan, museums, galleries and libraries, the post and telegraph, French railways and health spas, and Russian organizations abroad. Articles dealt with legislation relative to émigrés, social insurance, taxes and regulations on trade and industry, the French court system and local administration, French law on family, marriage and divorce, visas, banking, and Russian life in France (church, societies, schools, sport, military obligations, Jewish organizations, Billancourt-Boulogne, Marseilles, Lyon).[9]

The Parisian émigré press helped knit together refugees scattered across five continents. *Latest News* and *Renaissance* were read in major cities and obscure hamlets around the world. This press continued the "thick magazine" tradition of informing its readers about the wide world beyond Russia, an educational enterprise of unprecedented worth now that the readers were living in that wide world. It also satisfied an insatiable thirst among the émigrés for news of the motherland. Refugees were constantly searching for "a sign," evidence for democratization of the Soviet System which would allow their return. Hope swelled for many that the hour was at hand when they learned of the Kronstadt uprising, or the New Economic Policy, or the Stalin Constitution.[10] They also took heart in reading about those exceptional individuals among them who enjoyed fame and good fortune in exile, artists like Chaliapin and Pavlova, engineers like Sarnoff and Sikorsky. And the émigré press provided a medium and some financial support for writers. For instance, Nina Berberova as a struggling young poet published a highly popular cycle of stories called the "Billancourt Fiesta," local color about an émigré neighborhood, in *Latest News*.[11]

Neighborhoods

Billancourt, an industrial district in the extreme southwest of Paris, was where Russian refugee life could be found in its most concentrated form. Establishments up and down several bustling streets proclaimed their services in the Russian language: grocery stores, restaurants, small hotels and boarding houses, service stations. Russian residents had their own kindergarten, bookstore, barber shop, laundry, clinic, dentist, and crude wooden Orthodox chapel.[12] The local Renault and Citroën factories hired thousands of Russians. Abel Gance's film studios were here and employed a few. How ironic that in later years Paris city authorities should rename the adjacent quai "Stalingrad."

Russian colonies also developed in two suburbs just across the Seine, Clamart and Meudon. There was an aristocratic enclave in Clamart, an aristocracy of education and culture, represented by the philosopher Berdiaev. Those in Meudon, as in Billancourt, were socially diverse.

Russians were scattered through the city proper; a few who regained their wealth could be found in the most exclusive and expensive quarter of Passy. But perhaps the largest number lived in the eighth arrondissement, which stretches from the Etoile eastward to the St. Lazare train station. The latter was a source of income for émigré porters and taxi drivers. Not far from the Etoile is rue Daru, and there, clustered around the Alexander Nevsky Cathedral, were Russian shops, restaurants, and a library, not as extensive as in Billancourt, but the spot that would draw more Russians periodically than any other in the city.

Working

A scholarly survey for the year 1926 found that 17,217 Russian émigrés were working in Paris and of that number 4,198 were women.[13] The jobs most frequently mentioned in all sources were those in the auto factories. From the middle to late twenties, Renault was employing more than 4,000 Russians, and Citroën, about 1,000.[14] These men were earning the equivalent of about $2 a day and were considered highly reliable workers. For comparison we may recall that Henry Ford had first begun to pay some of his workers $5 a day back in 1914. Nina Berberova remarks that most of the Russian auto workers had been high ranking White Army officers. Their profound opposition to strikes, docility toward the law and the police, and reputations as good family men endeared them to their employers.[15]

The émigré job *par excellence*, often too for White Army veterans, was that of taxi driver. Such men would frequently advertise their origins by painting the emblem of the Russian bear on the sides of their cabs. In the prosperous twenties there were 3,000 Russian taxi drivers in Paris, and they could clear 100 francs ($4) per day. (That figure fell to forty to sixty francs for a twelve-hour day in the depressed thirties.)[16] The manifest independence of taxi driving, the possibility of genuine self-employment, made this a particularly attractive occupation. The city did impose a stiff examination, and many candidates took it three or four times before passing. One had to demonstrate driving skills and detailed acquaintance with the streets of Paris. But then one enjoyed extraordinary independence and respect from the public. A few Russian entrepreneurs offered satellite services, courses in driving and minor auto repairs and instruction in the city street pattern. French authorities provided space for workshops, and Renault donated their vehicle factory manuals. The Russian National University in Paris and several private auto schools offered driving instruction and maintained facilities for car washing, lubrication, and engine and chassis adjustment. When, however, the labor Ministry forbade foreigners from taking the taxi driver qualifying exam in the spring of 1926, the heyday of opportunity for would-be cabbies was ended.[17]

Tatiana Metternich, recalling her family life in the late twenties, noted that "Many of Mamma's guests had become taxi drivers, or were employed in similar jobs. They joked about their work as if it had nothing at all to do with their real life." Such a family friend was Valerian Bibikoff who one summer chauffeured a newly rich South American couple through Europe. While in Austria they happened to be staying in the same vicinity as King Alfonso XIII of Spain, and Bibikoff and the king spent several evenings together. Alfonso had been Honorary Commander of Bibikoff's Imperial Russian Guards Regiment. Bibikoff firmly resisted his employers' evident desire for an introduction to the king, holding that they were "not the sort of people" with whom Alfonso would have been comfortable.[18] The typical émigré defined himself in terms of what he had been before the revolution. His subsequent occupations mattered little regarding his sense of status.

Some eighty surviving members of one Cossack regiment all worked as porters at the Gare de l'Est. Several of the officers were reported to have refused better jobs in order to stay with their men. They lived together in wooden barracks decorated in the Cossack style. There were preserved photos, arms, uniforms, decorations, and the precious regimental flag. In the evenings the commandant colonel used to put away his porter's smock and don his uniform of short Cossack blouse and leather belt. "His former life resumes now and will last until morning, his real life. He rediscovers his personality, his friends, his country's atmosphere."[19]

Those self-employed as shopkeepers or artisans generally led a precarious existence. There was always a danger of their running afoul of French regulations. The Armenian Petrossian brothers' delicatessen, however, was an exceptional success story. With considerable effort they inculcated a taste for caviar in the French public and have thrived ever since. Petrossian S.A. is currently opening new outlets in the United States and several other countries.

Russian women commonly engaged in dressmaking or embroidery. In fact, émigré influence on the Paris fashion world was significant. Three thousand of them, mostly women, were employed in every phase of the business in 1926. A large majority, seventy-five percent of those so occupied, made from 400 to 600 francs a month. Top earners, including models, could make up to 2,000 francs a month. Living expenses in Paris those days ran from 1,000 to 1,500 francs per month for two people.[20] Paris supported over 100 small Russian dressmaking shops. Countess Orlov-Davydov managed a "Maison de Mode" not far from the rue Daru. The Grand Duchess Marie embroidered Russian-style blouses on commission to Coco Chanel and later opened her own embroidery factory, "Kitmir" which was quite successful for several years.[21] The skills of the seamstress were essential to the financial survival of many émigré families.

Soviet Surveillance

Soviet authorities monitored émigré activities with the keenest interest and long considered the exile community a dangerous opposition force. Communist agents successfully infiltrated all politically oriented White organizations and enjoyed considerable success in neutralizing them. Such spies built up detailed dossiers with accurate information about White organizations, their meeting places, and their leaders.[22] A Soviet press statement of September 1922 pinpointed Paris as a hot-bed of anti-communism: "In no other country than France, and in no capital but Paris, do the émigrés exert such enormous influence on government policies."[23] In the same period, Foreign Affairs Commissar George Chicherin declared that "The organizations of Russian emigrants now existing abroad are, in every case, counter-revolutionist groups spending the funds at their disposal to provoke attack against the territory of the Soviet Republic." [24] During the Stalinist purges of the 1930s, White émigrés were blamed for sabotaging the five-year plans, and hundreds of Old Bolsheviks who were condemned in the public trials were accused of complicity with the "White Guard reactionaries."

The OGPU (Unified State Political Administration), the Soviet secret police, set up a front organization which came to be known as "The Trust" and which operated effectively from 1924 into 1926. Purporting to be a powerful band of anti-communists inside the U.S.S.R., the Trust "virtually monopolized all undercover contacts between the U.S.S.R. on the one hand and the White para-military organization and their western friends on the other. "[25] Two notorious anti-communists, the terrorist Boris Savinkov and the spy Sydney Reilly (Russian-born as Zigmund Grigorievich Rosenblum), were lured into Soviet territory and to their deaths through the machinations of the Trust. While it lasted the Trust was phenomenally successful. "At one time the sums of money received from Western intelligence sources in payment for the 'information' supplied through the Trust were large enough to cover, not only the operational expenses of the entire Counter-Intelligence Department of the OGPU, but even some of the Foreign Department's own espionage activities abroad!"[26]

One formidable champion of the White cause remained. Lieutenant General Pavel Kutepov had been Wrangel's second in command in the last period of the civil war. A man of great integrity, energy, and physical courage, he had maintained strict discipline and kept up the morale of the White troops during their months of internment on Gallipoli and Lemnos. Kutepov later headquartered in Paris was in charge of the White veteran organizations and all undercover activities inside the U.S.S.R. He was a man of passion and saw the struggle with communism in purely military terms. His efforts did result in occasional acts of sabotage inside the Soviet Union. As Stalin's power was concentrated, the OGPU was directed to end these annoyances.

One Sunday morning in January 1930, General Kutepov set out from his home at 10:30 a.m. to walk to church services. He never arrived at his destination. A kidnapping was suspected, and 400 agents of the Paris and security police were put to work on the case. By piecing together eyewitness accounts, they arrived at the following scenario. Just one block from his apartment, Kutepov was spirited into a powerful, grayish-green Alfa-Romeo by two men, with an accomplice in gendarme's uniform as lookout. Followed by backups in a red Renault taxicab they sped across Paris. At the Pont de l'Alma, stopped in a traffic jam, the kidnapper, posing as a gendarme, explained to a passerby that he was administering an ether-soaked handkerchief to an "accident victim" whose legs had been crushed. The cars proceeded to the coast near Cabourg. From the Alfa, men carried a "longish package rolled up in sacking" down to the beach to a waiting launch. The package was transferred to a cargo vessel riding at anchor farther out to sea. That vessel was almost certainly the Soviet *Spartak* which in fact docked briefly at Antwerp the day after Kutepov's disappearance and then went on to Leningrad.

The Soviets did not admit culpability, but they were condemned in the French press, and voices were raised demanding that France break diplomatic relations with the Soviet Union. The general's disappearance was a cause célèbre for several weeks, with outraged French denunciations of the Soviet government for having authorized a brazen and criminal kidnapping in the middle of Paris in broad daylight. One evening 3,000 angry demonstrators marched on the Soviet Embassy. Then other international concerns loomed large, such as the developing economic crisis and Japanese aggression in Manchuria, and the affair was forgotten. Agents of the OGPU certainly did seize Kutepov, to eliminate an effective leader of the White opposition and, possibly, to force from him a repudiation of his past actions (as had come from Savinkov). But given his weak heart, the ether may have killed Kutepov minutes after he was seized.[27]

Lieutenant General Evgenny Miller replaced Kutepov. A more reflective man than his predecessor, Miller had a much less sanguine view. His policy was to act with caution, avoid embarrassing the allied Powers, and help his men to survive the Depression. But in time, Miller too disappeared.

Miller had reason to suspect one of his aides, General Nikolai Skoblin, of being an NKVD agent. (In 1934 the Soviet secret police were reorganized into the NKVD [People's Commissariant for Internal Affairs]). In September, 1937, Skoblin insisted that Miller meet with him and two alleged German agents at a quiet, residential address not far from the Bois de Boulogne. Miller reluctantly agreed but left a note for his deputy expressing his misgivings that Skoblin might be setting a trap. Miller never returned. The subsequent police investigation revealed that a gray Ford van owned by the Soviet Embassy had been observed parked one block from General Miller's rendezvous, at just about the time he was due there, 12:30 p.m. The van was parked in front of a Soviet-owned villa. In the late afternoon of the day Miller vanished, that same gray van arrived at the Le Havre docks. A heavy wooden packing case was put on board the steamer, *Maria Ulyanova*, and she weighed anchor that evening for Leningrad.

So once again circumstantial evidence strongly suggested the NKVD had boldly struck in the heart of Paris. Skoblin too disappeared that same day and was never seen again. By 1937 the French were becoming somewhat inured to political violence, which was increasing with the rise of fascism, so this affair was not the shock that the Kutepov disappearance had been. What turned into a cause célèbre was the trial of Skoblin's wife,

Nadezhda Plevitskaya. She was a popular concert artist, having sung on numerous tours throughout Europe and the United States. In December 1938 she was put on trial for conspiring with her husband (still vanished) to kidnap General Miller. Plevitskaya with great emotion refused to admit guilt or to implicate Skoblin. The press followed these proceedings avidly. In the end the accused was found guilty of "arbitrary sequestration and violence" and given an unusually severe sentence, twenty years at hard labor. Two years later Plevitskaya died, in the Rennes prison for women.

One may speculate that Miller fell to the NKVD, not only because he headed the White Army veterans, but because he knew too much about the NKVD. The Whites had their underground agents too who reported to Miller. There were rumors that the general was spirited into the U.S.S.R. alive (he was seventy years of age), but his fate is unknown. Soviet authorities steadfastly denied involvement in either the Kutepov or the Miller affair until a September 22, 1964, *Krasnaya zvezda (Red Star)* article referred to State Security's "brilliant operation in the arrest of Kutepov."[28] These two cases were the dramatic high points in the ongoing struggle between communist authorities and "White Guard reactionaries." The kidnappings of Kutepov and Miller were particularly demoralizing for the émigrés, and the Soviets' relentless harassment succeeded in nullifying effective expressions of White hostility.

EMIGRES IN NEW YORK

The Orthodox Church

When Whites began landing on U.S. shores, they found a network of Orthodox churches already in place. Russian colonizers of Alaska and California had introduced the first churches, and the predominantly peasant immigrants from Nicholas II's empire had supported a slowly expanding network. For 1916, Census Bureau figures record 169 Russian Orthodox churches in the United States with a membership of 99,681.[29]

Archbishop Platon of New York had organized the Russian Orthodox Immigration Society prior to the First World War. The Society maintained a "Russian Immigrant Home" on East Fourteenth Street which provided temporary shelter for some of the White refugees. Platon's St. Nicholas Cathedral, Fifth Avenue and Ninety-seventh Street, cooperated closely with the American Red Cross to transfer 2,041 Russians from Constantinople to the United States. The newcomers arrived in 1922 and 1923, and they settled for the most part in New York City. This particular group clearly owed a good deal to the Church.[30]

Mirroring what happened in Europe, the Church in America divided into splinter groups, reflecting political and ethnic divisions. Patriarch Tikhon in Moscow and an All-American Church Council named Archbishop Platon to be Primate of America in 1922. His leadership was challenged, however, by a Canadian bishop, Adam Philipovsky, who headed a Carpatho-Russian group of parishes. (The Carpatho-Rus were Slavic peoples who had emigrated from the territory of the former Austro-Hungarian Empire.) On one occasion, Adam and his followers barricaded themselves inside St. Nicholas Cathedral, claiming it for their own. A furious Platon and his supporters stormed the building wielding clubs and axes; they broke through the outer door before being repulsed. The U.S. courts upheld Platon, though, and Adam was imprisoned for thirty days.[31] After several years had passed, the Carpatho-Rus did agree to return to the fold.

But a permanent split followed Archbishop Platon's declaration of independence from Patriarch Tikhon in Moscow. Although an American Church Council confirmed Platon's legitimacy, he was challenged in the American courts by Ivan Kedrovsky. Kedrovsky represented the Soviet-sponsored "Living Church," was loyal to Moscow, and won his case in court. He thereby gained control of the much-contested St. Nicholas Cathedral. Since that 1925 court decision, there have been a small number of Orthodox churches in America, like St. Nicholas, which function directly under the authority of the Moscow patriarch.

Platon set up a new cathedral church on East Houston Street, a major area of Russian settlement in the city going back to prewar times. Sympathetic Episcopalians proffered a chapel for his use in their Houston Street Trinity Episcopal Church. Following the example of Metropolitan Eulogy in Paris, Platon also broke with the Yugoslavian-based Synod Abroad, that most militantly anti-communist group of ecclesiastics. The large majority of American churches were loyal to Platon, but quite a few aligned themselves with the Synod abroad. The latter were especially supported by the White refugees, and these churches in the United States are commonly styled "The Russian Orthodox Church Outside Russia." So by the end of 1926 there were three distinct jurisdictions: Platon's "Metropolia," the largest, with multi-ethnic members whose roots lay in Eastern Europe, the Balkans, and old Russia; the Russian Orthodox Church Outside Russia, the "White" bastion and self-consciously anti-Soviet; a few churches of the "Patriarchal Exarchate" loyal to Moscow. The dissensions among the faithful that these splits fomented primarily affected the prewar émigrés rather than the Whites.

The 2,041 Whites who came over from Constantinople were the core of post-revolutionary émigrés who settled in New York City. They established themselves in Harlem, centering near Fifth Avenue and 125th Street. Over several years they built their own church, Christ the Savior, at 51 East 121st Street. This became a focal point of the community which soon boasted three Russian bookstores and five Russian restaurants. The

American Episcopal Church especially supported these newcomers, and they were given use of the St. Andrew's Episcopal Church in Harlem for "Russian nights" of singing, dancing and dramatic performances.[32] Episcopalians also financially contributed to the building of Christ the Savior Church.

The number of Orthodox churches in the United States increased during the 1920s and 1930s although the total membership apparently did not. Commerce Department statistics, which may be incomplete, list a total of 229 churches with 89,510 members in 1936.[33] White refugees established a number of new churches and were active in some of the old ones. Involvement in the Church became essential to the lives of most White émigrés, but they did not mix easily with the masses of earlier, basically peasant, Orthodox parishioners.

The Emigré Press

The Russian press in the United States was a small segment of the foreign language press which had grown extensively during the prewar years of massive immigration. These publications were most vigorous during the First World War, and then they went into decline as "Americanization" became the watchword and immigration quotas were imposed. The Russian-language periodical press was controlled by special interests such as the Orthodox church, political factions, trade unions, or immigrant societies. Bitter infighting among press editors had exacerbated divisions within the Russian community. This "contributed to the isolation of Russian immigrants...from each other ... and from American society in general, especially during the period 1907-1914."[34] During the interwar years, Russian-language periodicals varied in number between twenty and thirty and continued to serve distinct groups that had formed form the earlier, peasant immigration.

Two New York newspapers are of particular interest. New World (Novyi mir) was Marxist. Bukharin and Trotsky (both to rival Stalin in the 1920s) briefly worked for it while chafing in the wilderness of exile. After the 1917 revolution, New World adopted an orthodox Bolshevik stance and remained stridently pro-Soviet until its demise in 1938. For example, its columnists in 1932 and 1933 were denouncing Trotsky (defeated by Stalin and once again in exile), attacking American socialists, calling on readers to vote Communist, and referring to FDR and his cabinet as the "bitterest enemies of the working class." Clearly, this was not the paper of choice for the White refugee community. New Russian Word (Novoe russkoe slovo) was much more to their taste. This anti-communist daily had the largest circulation of Russian-language periodicals and was the broadest in orientation.

New Russian Word is still the major Russian-language newspaper in the United States today, and it has been providing general national and international news, with particular attention to events inside the Soviet Union, and advice to immigrants about the peculiarities of life in the United States. As was also true of the major Parisian papers, *New Russian Word* included a section on literature and the arts. Its format and advertisements paralleled those of the Parisian émigré papers. There were notices of courses taught in Russian on academic and practical subjects. Opportunities to study English were listed. Names of missing persons and pleas for information about them appeared regularly. Retail shops of all kinds advertised, as well as restaurants, theaters, Russian bookstores, and banks dealing in rubles and prepared to transmit money or food parcels to the U.S.S.R. Physicians and lawyers and various émigré clubs and societies gave notice of their services and functions.

Through *New Russian Word*, one could keep abreast of cultural events, films, meetings, and lectures that would interest "American Russia," as the emigration in its entirety called. The "Women's Corner" featured articles on subjects like homemaking, fashion, and cosmetics. Tips on health and hygiene frequently appeared. Classified columns offered the Russian speaking housing and jobs. There were many articles on American customs and institutions. For the neophyte capitalist, there was a column on finances and the stock market. More narrowly focused Russian-language periodicals also carried many such ads and listings, performing a very important practical service.

The Russian-language press in the United States was modest in scope. There were no publishing houses as in Paris or Prague, but a newcomer could find something to read in his own language which would convey sympathetic understanding for his homesickness and his bewilderment in a strange land. One of the White refugees, Michael Argus, became a journalist for *New Russian Word*. In his view, "The newspaper is the pivotal center of a Russian's American life....It is simultaneously an information bureau, a first-aid station, an arbitration office, a broker, a general factotum, and intermediary between the Russian colony and the outside English-speaking world."[35]

Neighborhoods

Before any White refugees came on the scene, New York City's Russian colony numbered about 60,000, characterized by *The New York Times* as "true Russians, not Jews or Lithuanians."[36] Many of them lived in the traditional immigrant neighborhoods of the lower East Side. Another area of Russian concentration was in the Brownsville section of Brooklyn. The first Russian women's organization in the U.S.A. was, it so happens, formed in Brownsville. Their aim was to support the women's "Battalion of Death" that was guarding the Winter Palace in 1917 while it was the seat of the Provisional Government. These prewar immigrants in their various districts of the city were typically poor, unassimilated, and untutored enthusiasts of Bolshevism. Ignorance of English and illiteracy were rife among them.

A new appendage of the older colony was formed when some 6,000 White émigrés established residence in the city.[37] In the early twenties particularly, they created a close-knit community, adhering to their church on East 121st Street and the nearby Russian restaurants, bookstores, and library. As if in deliberate defiance, an office of the Young Workers Communist League was located four blocks from Christ the Savior Church. Already by the end of the decade there was a noticeable loosening of ties. Another Russian Orthodox Church had been built in the preponderantly Jewish Brownsville section. People began moving out to scattered areas and involving themselves more in American culture.

Working

Although the White émigrés were a highly educated group and largely professional people, nine-tenths of them began to support themselves in New York City through unskilled labor. They worked for the National Biscuit Company and candy factories, for Horn and Hardart and drug stores. *The New York Times* reported in 1923 that forty percent of recent Russian émigrés wished to become auto mechanics. Many were attending the West Side YMCA Auto School and believed that such skills would be valuable in the future Russia to which they hoped to return.[38] The émigré taxi drivers formed a Mutual Aid Society in 1928. Many others found employment in restaurants as waiters, waitresses, cooks, and dishwashers. There were milliners, housepainters, paperhangers, janitors, and construction workers. In 1924 the *Times* carried a story on White Russians with the heading, "Title and Talent, Exiled Toil Here in Lowly Tasks." Twenty men, "none with a title lower than captain," were reported to be working in one hospital. The writer observed with sly satisfaction that "A supreme court judge who once sent Jewish violators of passport regulations into exile is now a porter at a Jewish children's home."[39]

Not too much time passed, though, before a good many émigrés moved up to more desirable occupations. Women became language teachers, nurses, and social workers. Men and women found their way to university and scholastic posts. Most of the Russian doctors and dentists eventually passed the necessary examinations and resumed their practices. Quite a few succeeded as engineers and in other technical occupations. When Igor Sikorsky started aircraft manufacturing, he relied almost wholly on Russian personnel, and the Russian colony (including many of the old immigration) raised $200,000 capital to invest in his operation.[40] The Association of Russian Painters and Artists comprised some seventy painters, sculptors, and decorators as members, all active in New York City. Their honorary president was the well-known Russian painter, Nicholas Roerich. The Nicholas Roerich Museum on West 107th Street still displays his paintings and collections. The Grand Duchess Marie, former proprietress of Kitmir in Paris, became a styling consultant to a New York couturiere. This overall success in careers was thanks to the necessary mastery of English and sometimes further education. New York émigrés did so well that the Simpson survey found "During the depression, the refugees appeared to suffer from unemployment less than other classes of the community."[41]

PARIS AND NEW YORK COMPARED

Russian exiles from the Soviet Union descended upon Paris and New York City during the same period, the early twenties. They were predominantly upper-class and well-educated people. Many of the men, who outnumbered women, had been imperial army officers or had fought in the ranks of the White Army. The émigrés established tightly knit communities in both cities, Billancourt in Paris, East Harlem in New York, and the Orthodox Church was the central institution of community life. Wherever they found themselves, the émigrés had to scramble for low-status, low-paying, insecure jobs, and many men and women had to seek wage work for the first time in their lives. The automobile and restaurant industries proved sources of jobs in both cities. Somehow, most people got by, tolerated their plight as temporary, and dreamed of "the return."

Paris and New York, though, were unquestionably different experiences for Russian refugees. Paris became home to 50,000; New York, a larger city, had to absorb only 6,000. The population of Paris was slowly declining, from 2,907,000 in 1920 to 2,830,000 in 1936; whereas New York's population was rapidly increasing, from 5,620,048 in 1920 to 7,454,995 in 1940.[42] The much larger number of émigrés in Paris were a genuinely self-sustaining community, and their cohesiveness was strengthened by their status as the leaders of the White refugees worldwide. Those in New York were more easily lost in the crowd. The 60,000 or so Russians already in New York were socially and politically alien to the incoming Whites and did not generally act to ease their acclimation.

In Paris the Orthodox Synod Abroad challenged the mainstream Eparchy, and in New York the same Synod challenged the mainline Metropolia. Only in New York, however, did the Soviet-sponsored "Living Church" gain a foothold. And throughout America the diversity of ethnic groups who embraced Orthodoxy complicated the organization of that Church. Paris was one of the major Russian-language publishing centers in the world; New York was not. But the pro-Communist New York newspaper, *New World,* had no counterpart in Paris. The émigrés in Paris were highly visible thanks to their large numbers and considerable cultural and political activities. The Whites in New York attracted no particular attention among the numerous immigrant groups living in that city.

The Soviet intelligence service regarded the Parisian exile community as a major anti-Soviet threat; New York was considered a backwater and was not disturbed by sensational kidnappings of prominent Whites. Emigrés were far more likely to find fashion-related occupations in Paris, since New York as yet counted for little in the world of fashion, before the advent of Claire McCardell. The Russians in Paris, however, were more likely to remain trapped in dead-end jobs. In New York, the much smaller colony could not be so self-contained; hence, refugees were prone to learn the native language more quickly. They were encouraged to naturalize, they did become U.S. citizens, and this helps explain the pattern of occupational upward mobility.

NOTES TO CHAPTER V

1. Quoted in Vladislavlev, (pseud.S. Kamenskii) *Iz Zapisnoi Knizhki Bezhentsa (From a Refugee's Notebook)* (Paris, 1963), 58-59.

2. Michael Hansson, pres. of the Nansen International Office, *Les réfugiés et leur sort* (1937), 20, in Goldenwiser, Box 12, Bakhmeteff Archive, Columbia University.

3. John Shelton Curtiss, *The Russian Church and the Soviet State* (Gloucester, MA, 1965), reprinted from 1953, 109.

4. Charles Ledré, *Les émigrés russes en France* (Paris, 1930), 234.

5. *Vozrozhdenia,* Paris daily, September 8, 1939.

6. W. Chapin Huntington, *The Homesick Million, Russia-out-of Russia* (Boston, 1933), 37.

7. A. Beloborodova, "Conditions de la vie des émigrés à Paris," *Russie et chrétienté,* No. 1 (1937), 108.

8. Huntington, 39.

9. V.A. Obolenskii and B.M. Sarach, eds., *Russkii al'manakh-spravochnik (Russian Almanac and Reference Book)* (Paris, 1931).

10. Comment by Mark Vishniak, an editor of *Contemporary Annals,* in his *Years of Emigration, 1919-1969,* Paris-New York (Stanford, CA, 1970), 52-53. The 1921 Kronstadt uprising was a major sailors' mutiny against communist party dictatorship. The NEP of the same year permitted a degree of private economic enterprise. The 1936 "Stalin Constitution" appeared to guarantee an impressive list of civil rights for citizens.

11. Nina Berberova, *The Italics are Mine* (New York, 1969), 353.

12. Huntington, 31.

13. Georges Mauco, "Les étrangers en France", doctoral dissertation (Paris, 1932), 300, 304.

14. Obolenskii and Sarach, 277.

15. Berberova, 332.

16. Andrei Sedykh (pseud.), Zwiback, Jacques, *Liudi za bortom (Men Overboard)* (Paris, 1933), 17-20.

17. *The Russian National University in Paris,* ca. 1931, 10, Association pour la conservation des valeurs culturelles russes, 1917-1947, 8 AS, 42, Archives nationales, Paris.

18. Tatiana Metternich, *Purgatory of Fools* (New York, 1976), 45-46.

19. Jean Delage, *La Russie en exil* (Paris, 1930), 64-68.

20. *Vozhrozhdenie* (Feb. 14, 1926), 4.

21. Marie, Grand Duchess of Russia, *A Princess in Exile* (New York, 1932), 165.

22. Maurice Friedberg, "USSR and its Emigrés," *Russian Review* 27 (Apr. 1968): 131-132.

23. Cited by Nadia Tongour, "Diplomacy in Exile: Russian Emigrés in Paris, 1918-1925," unpub. Ph.D. dissertation (Stanford University, 1979), fn. 207, p. 501.

24. *Russian Refugees, General Correspondence*, Russia, WWI, 948.62, American National Red Cross Archives, Washington, D.C.

25. Geoffrey Bailey (pseud.), *The Conspirators* (New York, 1960), 13.

26. Ibid., 67. "The Trust" is reviewed in Teodor Gladkov & Nikolai Zaitsev, *I ia emu ne mogu ne verit'* . . ., 2nd ed. (Moscow, 1986), 72-106.

27. Bailey, 89-117.

28. Ibid., 234-266. Red Star quote in John J. Dziak, *Chekisty - A History of the KGB* (Lexington, MA, 1988), 99.

29. Statistics cited by Jerome Davis, *The Russian Immigrant* (New York, 1922), 91.

30. Basil M. Bensin, *History of the Russian Orthodox Greek Catholic Church of North America* (New York, 1941), 17-19.

31. Ivan K. Okuntsov, *Russkaia emigratsiia v severnoi i iuzhnoi Amerike (Russian Immigrants into North and South America)* (Buenos Aires, 1937), 139-140.

32. *New York Times*, (Feb. 8, 1925), x, 10, and (Apr. 12, 1925), iv., 20.

33. Cited by Bensin, 31.

34. Robert A. Karlowich, "The Russian-Language Periodical Press in New York City from 1889 to 1914," unpubl. D. Lib. Sci. dissertation (Columbia University, 1981), 498-499.

35. Michael K. Argus, *Moscow-on-the-Hudson* (New York, 1948), 32.

36. Number estimated in "Beat Bolshevism in Its Best Field," *New York Times* (Dec. 28, 1919), ii., p. 2.

37. Figures for White Russians in New York City taken from Sir John Hope Simpson, *The Refugee Problem* (London, 1939), 469.

38. *New York Times* (Dec. 30, 1923), viii, p. 2.

39. Ibid. (Sept. 28, 1924), vii, p. 15.

40. Okuntsov, 308.

41. Simpson, 471.

42. Paris figures from *European History Statistics*, 1750-1975, 2nd rev. ed. (New York, 1989), Index B4, p. 88. New York City figures from *Population Abstract of the United States* (McLean, VA, 1983), 548.

VI. Exile Community Organizations and Services

Russian émigrés in the 1920s created an extraordinary number of associations for mutual aid and support. They joked among themselves that the typical exile belonged to five or ten Russian organizations. The tendency to form ethnic enclaves is, of course, common to all immigrant groups. But the White émigrés in their first years of exile felt extraordinarily vulnerable and in need of each other. They had not chosen to leave their native land, and they were not quick to identify with a new one. Feeling themselves to be in a holding pattern until they could return to home ground, they clung closely together to weather their uncharted course. The resulting associations concerned every sphere of life: social, cultural, political, and economic.

Even without formal organization, émigrés were gregarious. Private homes have always been favorite meeting places for Russian socializing and this continued to be true in exile. Several prominent families were able to transplant a characteristically Russian institution to French soil, the *usad'ba* (country estate). Two of these were in suburbs southwest of Paris. Pierre Kovalevsky has described his family's estate in Meudon where 2,000 Russian émigrés lived. The father of the family, Evgraf P. Kovalevsky, had been an educational expert in Imperial Russia, and he was noted for his educational and social activities in France between the wars. The Kovalevsky home in Meudon was a grand old villa that had once belonged to Moliere's wife. It could accommodate more than 100 guests at one time, and there were ample grounds which included a large tennis court. What made this an *usad'ba* was its openness to guests: Russians, French, and other nationalities were constantly being received. Many people came to use the library. In short, the place was a social and cultural center.

Nearby in the aristocratic enclave of Clamart was the Prince Grigory Troubetskoi estate, with a rambling house in extensive grounds and a small Orthodox chapel that the prince built to accommodate the neighboring Russians. Troubetskoi lived like an old-fashioned Russian landowner and presided over a circle of some 300 people, the cream of Russian émigré society. A third such estate was "Petrovka," close to Marseilles, the domain of the Tian-Shanskii family.[1] A portrait by Ilya Repin of the family's celebrated forebear, Semenov-Tian-Shanskii, still hangs in the Leningrad State Russian Museum. Nicholas II conferred the honorary surname "Tian-Shanskii" upon Semenov in recognition of his pioneering mountain explorations. Semenov's important work was on the formidable Tian Shan range which arises just east of Tashkent and thrusts into China. The Tian-Shanskiis, like the Troubetskois and Kovalevsky, represented pre-revolutionary Russian high society. They all endeavored to maintain open houses where a diversity of guests could feel at ease in an informal setting.

WHITE ARMY VETERANS

The Russian Armed Services Union (commonly referred to by its Russian acronym, "ROVS") was the largest and most visible exile organization. It was established by Baron Wrangel, the last commander of the White Army. He saw it as a veterans' organization to maintain the discipline and esprit of his troops and as a counterpoise to the Communist International. Members of ROVS, also popularly known as the Volunteer Army, could perhaps one day be mobilized to resume the armed struggle against the Bolshevik regime. A few émigrés doubted the wisdom of maintaining such a military organization. In 1921, for instance, Miliukov's *Latest News* opposed continuation of the Volunteer Army as based on illusion. Such a weak force, the argument ran, could not mount a viable challenge to Soviet strength.[2]

Practically all of the 60,000 White Army veterans, however, faithfully manned the ranks of the Volunteer Army for the remainder of their lives. The organization was made up of eight departments, five in Europe, two in America, and one in the Far East. Headquarters were in Paris. The avowed goal was to assume leadership of an internal uprising against communism. The practical function was to give veterans unwavering assurance of their worth and dignity as well as more tangible forms of support. Local organizations were typically regimental, with a core of officers who had served in combat together or who had graduated from the same school. One such solid and active group was the Paris-based Association of Russian Naval Officers. Most politically minded émigrés favorably regarded the Volunteer Army, for in it they saw a powerful symbol of the true Russian state, concrete evidence that authentic Russia still survived.

The Russian Armed Services union offered an impressive array of services to its members. It operated employment bureaus, legal aid offices, and evening schools. (The usual subjects were military science and Russian history.) It paid transportation costs for men seeking work and could also help with passports and visas. Local veterans' clubs frequently had their own library, meeting hall, and chapel. Unremitting effort went into fund raising for needy and disabled veterans.

When the Russian civil war ended, about 6,000 disabled veterans made their way to Europe with some 600 settling in France. They formed their own Russian Disabled Veterans Association. As veterans aged, the invalid ranks were joined by those who fell prey to accident or ill health.

The invalid soldier was an object of particular compassion. From 1926 the Volunteer Army sponsored an annual "Day of the Invalid," a day of ceremonies within the exile community to solicit donations for disabled veterans. By the late 1930s the largest private sums were being raised in the United States. In 1938, for example, the White Russian, San Franciscan contingent raised $4,000 for invalids through their annual charity ball. The following year at a comparable Paris ball the equivalent of about $1,500 was collected.[3] A good part of these sums went to maintain invalid veterans in nursing homes, over 1,000 of whom were being cared for in Europe in 1939. The most substantial contributions and some medical services came from European governments. The League of Nations Nansen Office gave annual donations as well. The Disabled Veterans Association was spending $15,000 to $20,000 a year in direct aid to invalids.

White veterans in New York belonged to one of the ROVS departments, and they formed their particular clubs, such as the Society of the Russian Imperial Guard, the Russian Naval Officers Group, and the Society for Aid to Invalids. These were the most influential émigré organizations in the United States, and they spearheaded drives to raise considerable sums which were largely spent in Europe.

POLITICS

The first years of exile were the most fraught with political activity. Two opposed political bodies were organized in Paris: The Russian National Committee on the right and the Republican-Democratic Union on the left. The leader of the Russian National Committee was A.V. Kartashev, an anti-communist and a staunch defender of the Volunteer Army. Here is a characteristic statement of the Committee's stand: "Absolute opposition to Bolshevism and merciless struggle until its complete destruction eliminates the possibility of any seductive compromises with the notorious achievements of Soviet power, with their military forces, diplomacy, economy, pseudo-nationalism, or other duplicity."[4] Miliukov led the Republican-Democratic Union which, although highly critical of the communist regime, did recognize some of the positive achievements made during its time in power. Émigrés did not tend to establish overtly political organizations, but their conscious alignment with either "right" or "left" meant that various associations split into opposed political groupings. Thus, there were divisions in the Church, and in Paris, two factions of disabled veterans, marines, engineers, lawyers, and academics.

In the United States, "old" immigrants supported a number of left–wing parties such as the Russian Federation of the Socialist Party of America or the anarchist Federation of Russian Workers. These were

eschewed by the White émigrés. The latter certainly did argue among
themselves about Russia and Bolshevism in the pattern of their fellow
exiles in Europe. But the exile community in New York did not fracture
over political differences; rather, their groupings tended to have left and
right wings but to remain unified. A parallel tolerance of aesthetic differences was notable in the Union of Russian Painters and Artists. Its members pursued styles that ranged from conservative academic realism
through impressionism to cubism. Desire for fellowship in the relatively
small New York colony overcame differences of opinion that would have
been divisive in other circumstances.

When Grand Duke Kirill Vladimirovich declared himself pretender to
the Russian throne in 1924, a small group of devotees formed the Russian
Legitimist-Monarchist Union to support his claim. Kirill was a first
cousin of the martyred Nicholas II, but even a good number of avowed
monarchists repudiated him. He was said to have betrayed his cousin
and sovereign by the unseemly haste with which he had sworn allegiance
to the Provisional Government in March 1917. And his wife was a
divorced woman and unrepentant Lutheran. In New York, the Russian
National Society in America, led by Boris Brasol, favored restoration of
the monarchy under Kirill, but very few Russian refugees concerned
themselves with the issue of a restored monarchy. Until his death in 1929,
Grand Duke Nicholas Nicolaevich, another cousin of Nicholas II, had his
champions who formed the Supreme Monarchist Council. Nicholas
Nicolaevich had been Commander-in-Chief of the Imperial Army for a
time but in his diffidence never formally asserted a claim to the throne.
Activities on the extreme right by a few monarchists had little impact on
the main body of the exile community.

A few émigrés openly expressed their admiration for fascism, but they,
too, were unrepresentative of the Whites and exerted no lasting influence. Alexander Kazem-Bek, of aristocratic Caucasian origin, founded
the "Young Russia" movement in Paris. He and his followers espoused
ardent nationalism, "solidarity" as opposed to class conflict, authority,
and ideals based on youthful enthusiasm rather than corrupt tradition.
"Young Russia", identified with the younger generation in the U.S.S.R.,
admired the strength of the Red Army, and placed their faith in a failure
of Marxism, which they hoped would be overthrown basically by internal revolt. This party remained aloof from other fascistic organizations in
Europe, even Russian ones in Germany, and is primarily of interest
because of the prickly and quixotic character of its founder, Kazem-Bek.

Even more quixotic was the White Army veteran, Anastase Vonsiatsky.
An American heiress brought him back to the United States and married
him, thus providing Vonsiatsky with the funds to found the "All-Russian
Fascist Organization." He put out a monthly paper, *Fashist*, distributed in
about 10,000 Russian-language copies, and he claimed to be leading a
vast organization with saboteurs and assassins operating to devastating

effect within the Soviet Union. All this was fantasy. There were in fact only half-a-dozen active Russian fascists on the east coast of the United States.[5] Vonsiatsky did travel to Europe and Asia, did meet other fascistically-inclined émigrés, and he did subsidize the reprinting of some of his articles abroad. But he was dismissed by men like Kazem-Bek as a lightweight adventurer, an unsavory gigolo, and a one-man show.

SOCIAL SERVICES

By far the greatest émigré organizational energy was expended in charitable work. The most extensive aid to émigrés was provided by their Union of Zemstvos and Towns (Zemgor). "Zemstvos" had been units of local government established in Russia after the 1861 emancipation of the serfs. For half a century members of the intelligentsia had willingly served in these zemstvos, utilizing what means they had to improve life in the countryside for the former serfs. During the First World War, zemstvos and municipal governments worked through a joint committee to support the war effort, and this joint committee came to be known as "Zemgor." Quite a few Zemgor activists went into exile and carried on the work of their organization from new headquarters in Paris. Prince G.E. Lvov, formerly president of Zemgor and president of the Provisional Government, resumed his leadership of Zemgor in Paris.

Zemgor was dedicated to relief work for Russian refugees. Initially the largest expenditures were in Constantinople, and most attention was paid to job placement. The money came from the American Red Cross, various European governments, the League of Nations, and Russian assets abroad. Zemgor set up employment bureaus in Paris, Marseilles, and Corsica. Out of 4,948 registrants, it placed 3,879 (seventy-eight percent) in jobs during 1921-1922.[6] Not only were individuals placed in already existing positions, but they could avail themselves of training courses, cooperatives, and craft outlets set up by Zemgor. Following naturally from its traditional concern with rural affairs, Zemgor published a bulletin aimed at neophyte refugee agriculturalists, primarily in France. The articles were a mixture of the technical and the general: "Notes on Viniculture;" "How to Become a Sharecropper"; "From the Life of Farmers in France"; "The Post Box." There was information on obtaining loans and commiseration about French language and food—how could one live without herring? Zemgor also ran a lending library which sent books to provincials through the mails.

As time went by, the resources of Zemgor were increasingly used to provide relief for refugee children. Needy children were given food, clothing, medical care, and support for education. By 1927, V.V. Rudnev reported, 95.8 percent of Zemgor funds were expended on aid to children. He summarized what the organization had done since the revolu-

tion: "organized or subsidized over 1,000 establishments such as : can-
teens providing cheap meals, night shelters, baths and laundries, hospitals, sanitoriums, and out-patient departments, workshops, labor and
employment bureaus, teaching of trades and crafts, legal aid, libraries
and reading rooms, popular universities, foreign language classes, children's asylums, kindergartens, summer camps, and a whole network of
elementary and secondary schools."[7] The following year Zemgor expended in direct aid to refugees 792,049 francs (about $31,000).[8]

Often cooperating with Zemgor and a substantial relief agency in its
own right was the Russian Red Cross. Patronized by the last two
empresses and thus closely associated with the imperial government, its
primary mission had been the care of wounded and ailing soldiers.
Russian Red Cross representatives had been active in allied countries
during the Great War, and when peace came they organized their own
chapters to serve their exiled countrymen. Medical aid continued to be
their top priority. They ministered especially to disabled veterans, children, and the elderly, and from 1921 to 1925, the Russian Red Cross
expended 24 million francs (on the order of $1,500,000).[9] Financial sup-
port came from the International Red Cross, from governmental and
international agencies, churches, and the émigrés themselves.

A Red Cross adoption agency placed hundreds of Russian orphans
with families. Medical aid frequently went to persons suffering from
tuberculosis, a disease rampant within the exile community at that time.
Through the considerable efforts of Red Cross volunteers, some Russian
émigrés gained admission to French hospitals. In 1930, Russian Red
Cross chapters around the world were maintaining three hospitals, a
tuberculosis sanitarium, twenty-six dispensaries, two old people's
homes, one home for invalids, three children's homes, four shelters, a
soup kitchen, and three refugee workrooms.[10] These operations were
entirely independent of the Soviet Red Cross organization which had
been set up in 1923 and was recognized by the International Red Cross.
The "Old" Russian Red Cross depended upon the services of Orthodox
nuns and extended help to them in various countries, including the
U.S.S.R. It was particularly active in Paris where its dispensary in 1935
served 11,793 people. Overall expenditures by the Russian Red Cross that
year were 4,849,728 francs (over $320,000).[11] On the eve of World War II,
the Russian Red Cross, like ROVS, was receiving its most generous support from America. The largest single donation in 1937 was $14,329, from
the American Society for the Relief of Russian Exiles.[12]

The Russian Red Cross had an office on lower Fifth Avenue in New
York City. Back in 1906 it had come under the control of militants who
concentrated their efforts on aiding political victims of the 1905 Russian
revolution. When the Whites started to arrive there were about 300 members of the New York chapter. It was reoriented to sympathize with the
new émigrés of the 1917 revolution, and under the presidency of M.

Bouimistroff, the New York chapter worked with such people as the Yusupovs to channel aid primarily to the needy refugees in Europe.

Charitable organizations associated with the Orthodox Church were active in support of the exile community. Working out of Metropolitan Eulogy's own rectory was the Women's Association of the rue Daru Russian Parish. A Russian Christian Labor Confederation was founded when France began to feel the effects of the depression. This Confederation repudiated the leftist sentiments and political activism of the major French unions; its motto was "Faith, Motherland, Family." It actively sought ties with French Christian syndicates. In 1933 there were 1,115 members of the Russian Confederation (calling themselves the "white proletariat"). There were 150,000 French members of the Christian syndicates. Emphasis in the Russian Christian Labor Confederation was clearly on services to members rather than collective bargaining. Loans, legal aid, unemployment compensation, and subsidies for children's camps and for vacations were characteristic benefits.[13]

Mother Marie (Skobtzova) had Eulogy's support in establishing "Orthodox Action." Prominent theologians such as Berdiaev, Bulgakov, and Fedotov took part in this vigorous enterprise geared to providing the most basic needs. Mother Marie presided over a dormitory in Paris for Russian female students which developed into a busy social center. She became a familiar figure in the very early mornings at Les Halles, and merchants often set aside some of their less desirable items for her at reduced prices. Thus she fed her charges. She was instrumental in founding a rest home outside Paris which housed thirty destitute Russians. Funds for "Orthodox Action," by the way, came in large part from non-Orthodox, frequently Anglican, sympathizers in places like London, Geneva, and New York. Mother Marie and her son, Yuri, a co-founder of Orthodox Action, were eventually arrested by the Gestapo for sheltering Jews. They and a fellow activist, Father Dimitri Klepinin, died in Nazi concentration camps.

In the United States, Archbishop Platon had organized the Russian Orthodox Immigration Society in 1908. The Society maintained an immigrant home on East 14th Street that offered temporary shelter to newcomers of Russian extraction. The Church had long encouraged fraternal organizations, mutual aid "brotherhoods" which typically paid death benefits ($250 to $1,000) to members. The Russian Orthodox Church in America also supported several welfare homes and orphanages, but all these activities primarily served the old immigration rather than the Whites.

In the closely knit world of the Russian émigrés there were a multitude of interconnections among charity organizers. Practically all the service organizations participated in common drives to fund the major and ongoing causes: disabled war veterans, needy children, the unemployed, and the homeless. The Paris community was particularly proud of the retirement home they developed in nearby Ste. Geneviève des-Bois. A chateau and several neighboring chalets housed upward of 300 men and women. Princess Mestchersky, one of the Russian Red Cross directors, founded the home with very generous financial support from a former pupil, Dorothy Paget. Ms. Paget had been an English student at the princess's finishing school, and she became immensely concerned with the sufferings of many émigrés. She inherited great wealth, bought the properties in St. Geneviève-des-Bois, and for a good many years made substantial donations to the home. She also saw to it that the residents were supplied with turkey and plum pudding at Christmas time.

A large number of the initial residents carried titles redolent of former days of glory: The Serene Princess Galitsin, widow of the Master of the Royal Hunt; Baron Knorring, equerry of the imperial court; Senator Andreevsky, governor of Orel and huntsman of the imperial court; M. Smourov, churchwarden of St. Isaac's Cathedral.[14] But the administration prided itself on admitting commoners as well, sometimes former servants, and in treating all residents alike. As time went on, more people of humble background were able to gain admittance.

Stepping inside the home was to be transported back to old Russia. The salon was dominated by a portrait of Empress Marie (mother of Nicholas II), and samovars gently burbled there for countless servings of tea. A gem of a chapel was done in Novgorod style with icons gleaming in candlelight. Portraits of Alexander II and Nicholas II presided over the dining room. Residents had their photographs, letters, books, and keepsakes, mementoes of a vanished world which adorned their simple, well-appointed rooms looking out onto the park. A visitor could catch murmurs of quiet conversation and observe a refined etiquette that evoked Russian drawing rooms of bygone times.

The thoroughgoing Russian atmosphere of typical émigré institutions is well described by Taya Zinkin when she recalls the nursing home that her father operated in Neuilly (just west of Paris where the famous American hospital is located): "The nurses were ex-army nurses, some of them veterans of up to three wars; the menials were disbanded Cossacks. To the very end, in 1939, father's nursing home remained a little Tsarist Russia embedded in the heart of France... Prince Galitzine [sic], the nursing home's cook, never quite forgot — nor did anybody else — that his ancestors had been Tsars long before the Romanoffs. This little world whose epicenters were firmly poised in the Russian Orthodox Church of the rue Daru and Petrossian's delicatessen was one in which the franc remained permanently subdivided into kopeks."[15] A champagne party was given to celebrate the grand opening of the home in May 1924. The Grand Duke Vladimir, the Yusupovs, and other dignitaries enjoyed such Russian delicacies as fresh black caviar, *piroshki* (dumplings), and *vatrouchki* (cheese cake), sturgeon steaks roasted on the spit, slices of sturgeon in aspic, and fresh pineapples bathed in kirsch.[16]

Comparable institutions in the United States were generally unpretentious, bearing the stamp of the old immigration. A notably active mutual aid organization was founded in Philadelphia in 1926, the Russian Consolidated Mutual Aid Society of America (ROOVA). ROOVA was explicitly anti-communist and had quite a few branches in New York, so although it was dominated by prewar immigrants, some of the Whites became members.[17] A women's chapter concerned with Balkan émigrés formed in New York. The Society's primary function was to provide health insurance and death benefits, but it expanded operations considerably further. A cooperative farm was developed on 1,400 acres purchased near Lakewood, NJ. The grounds were also used as a winter holiday resort and as a summer children's camp. The directors had plans for a retirement home which in fact was built after the Second World War. Several hundred members worked plots during the depression years, thus somewhat alleviating the hardships of unemployment. In the mid-thirties, ROOVA's directors pleaded for all Russian immigrants to pull together and try to forget past differences. They extended an olive branch to the Whites, suggesting that it was time to drop the appellation "new immigration" for those who came over after 1917. They reassured skeptics that very few of those "who landed in America in 1923" had enjoyed unearned income and were on the contrary accustomed to work.[18] Limited intermingling occurred, although the different immigrant waves never lost their distinctions.

Leo Tolstoy's youngest daughter, Alexandra, landed in San Francisco in 1931. She settled on the East Coast and with the support of prominent émigrés was able to launch the Tolstoy Foundation in 1939. Its purpose was to assist any refugees anywhere, and among the early patrons were Boris A. Bakhemeteff, erstwhile Russian Provisional Government Ambassador to the United States, Igor Sikorsky, Sergei Rachmaninov, and Tatiana Tolstoy. During the war years the Foundation sent provisions to some of the Russian prisoners in Europe. Since then it has enabled many thousands of Russians and refugees of all nationalities to settle permanently.[19]

Intellectuals among the New York émigré group maintained a fund that extended aid to a good many of the intelligentsia. The Literary Fund was under the direction of Mark E. Veinberg and made grants and loans to writers, journalists, scholars, and scientists in exile worldwide. Through regular appeals, charity concerts, and balls, over $60,000 was raised and distributed during the interwar period.[20] Both Nina Berberova and Mark Vishniak were among writers who have acknowledged modest sums from the Literary Fund coming to themselves or their friends.

The plight of children was always of foremost concern. In a meeting at the 125th Street YMCA, members of Harlem's Russian enclave founded the Russian Emigrant Children's Welfare Society (Obshchestvo Pomoshchi Detiam Russko Emigratsii). From its origin in 1926, the chief aim of the society was to give financial and material support to orphanages, schools, camps, and hospitals for children. A dozen chapters across the United States and Canada developed with steadily increasing participation and donations. Each chapter enjoyed considerable autonomy, and several assumed special obligations. The California group, who had come mostly through the Far East, made a point of supporting shelters in Shanghai and Harbin. The St. Louis chapter was committed to funding a summer camp in Bulgaria. The Society as a whole provided some funds to an orphanage in South Canaan, Pennsylvania, but most of the aid went abroad, to the Far East, Eastern Europe, and the Baltic States, and to France and Germany. Through a "Godparent" program, individuals could support a particular child for the sum of $10 a month. Seventy-eight godchildren were being cared for in 1941. By that time the Society had expended a total of over $110,000 on direct aid to children.[21]

The "Day of the Russian Child" was an annual holiday that émigrés in Europe celebrated as a fund raiser for child welfare. The Russian Emigrant Children's Welfare Society introduced this observance into America in 1932. Benefit performances, lectures, and church services raised significant contributions for child welfare in both Europe and America. These activities aimed to feed starving children and also to unite them and to give them through community support love of their motherland and pride in their nation.

EDUCATION AND YOUTH ORGANIZATIONS

In the mid-twenties Zemgor established that 18,000 to 20,000 Russian children of school age in western Europe required systematic financial support.[22] Primary schools in France were free to refugee children, but their families often could not provide their basic needs. A Paris school report on Russian children noted that "The parents of the pupils, employed in factories, usually herd together in third-rate hotels that are dirty, chilly and unsanitary. Families of four or five members live together in one room. Usually no heating exists on those premises."[23] Zemgor files are full of references to hunger, anemia, tuberculosis, inadequate clothing, disintegration of the home, and premature smoking and drinking by the most refractory children. The great majority of émigré children attended French schools, but many parents feared "denationalization" and endeavored to send their children to Russian schools staffed by Russian teachers. Zemgor was the major source of financial support for these institutions. During the interwar period it subsidized seventy-five to eighty Russian schools, at primary and secondary levels, across Europe. At least 6,000 children received educational help in this way. Fifteen to thirty percent of the pupils in these schools were orphans.[24]

The Central Committee for Patronage of Russian University Youth raised the equivalent of $10,000,000 to help 8,000 Russian refugees attain higher education degrees. The Patronage Committee worked very closely with Zemgor and solicited funds throughout the exile community and from every conceivable public and private agency. Most generous of individual patrons was the Dutch oil magnate, Sir Henry Deterding, who contributed 1,500,000 francs and established 100 scholarships for Russian students in European universities. Renowned as chairman of Royal Dutch Shell and one of the forgers of an international oil cartel, Deterding was married to a Russian. His wife's compassion for her people, as well as his anti-communism, moved Deterding to be magnanimous. Koussevitzky, Rachmaninov, and Pavlova were among other notable donors.[25]

The Patronage Committee subsidized hundreds of university students in France in various ways. It prevailed upon the government to grant some of them tuition exemption. The government also allowed students on stipends to travel by rail for half-fare. Most importantly, the Committee awarded monthly scholarships during the academic year, ranging from fifty to 350 francs. The sums were deliberately less than the cost of living, in order to extend them to the maximum number of students and to require that students work and save money. It was thought salutary to aid only the most committed who were willing to sacrifice. The Committee provided books and other materials to needy students. It also subsidized boarding houses, including two in Paris that accommodated eighty students. A few found work as tutors, but most labored at menial tasks; they were dog-walkers, errand boys, window-washers, porters, assistant store clerks, etc.

Michael M. Federov, a former commerce minister in the Imperial Government, directed the Patronage Committee with wholehearted commitment. He kept personally in touch with a great many students and tirelessly campaigned on their behalf. He made the most of the fact that Raymond Poincaré and Alexandre Millerand, two successive presidents of France, were both supporters and defenders of Russian refugees. In general, government authorities believed that it was in the French interest to help educate Russian students. The French and the Russians anticipated that those students would one day return to the Soviet Union; they would presumably remain grateful to France for their educations and always be sympathetic to the nation which had harbored them.

Some exiles began to question as early as 1923 whether or not there would be a "return," but that promise remained an article of faith for the Patronage Committee. Illustrating this are a number of Federov's official statements: "Well aware of the great requirements of future Russia, after its liberation, and its need for technical specialists of all kind to reconstruct the ruined Nation, the majority of Russian students are trying to enter technical schools." (1930). Russian youth "are preparing to serve their country worthily the day of Russia's liberation from the communist yoke." (1933). We are preparing "new Russian cultural forces for future Russia, when she is freed from the communist yoke." (1936). "It is evident to everyone that the end of the communist regime and the regeneration of national Russia are approaching". (1938).[26] Since most students were not in fact returning, Federov's committee sent out hundreds of recommendation letters to prospective employers. Charged with Federov's zeal, this was an outstandingly beneficial exile organization.

The French people's concern for young Russian refugees was best expressed through *L'Union française d'aide aux Russes*. Like the Patronage Committee, this body awarded grants to university students ranging from fifty to 350 francs per month. The Union stood ready to bail out students faced with unexpected expenses, for books, clothing, examination fees, or medical costs. It helped hundreds of young émigrés to get through secondary schools as well, by offering scholarships or helping to arrange for reduced tuition. And the Union lent its good offices to place some 400 émigré children into orphanages or youth shelters.[27]

An American group also helped to sustain some of the Russian university students in France. American archaeologist and Byzantinist, Thomas Whittemore, founded the Committee for the Education of Russian Youth in Exile. His interest stemmed from his relief work with Russian war refugees. From his home base in Boston he focused on their educational needs. Whittemore appealed to wealthy Americans who sympathized with the victims of communism, and his committee expended over $300,000 to aid Russian students throughout Europe. Koussevitzky and Rachmaninoff were sponsors of Whittemore's committee, exemplifying how it interconnected with Federov's Patronage Committee. Following a popular American approach, supporters were invited to "adopt" a student, and Rachmaninoff did so. One of the composer's protégés, Paul Milovanoff, was enabled to finish his work at the University of Sofia and to take up postgraduate studies in chemistry at the Haute Ecole de Chimie, in Nancy, France.[28] A small number of graduates were returning to the U.S.S.R. and Whittemore noted in 1926 that Soviet authorities acknowledged the work of his committee and had expressed the need for young scientists and technicians. He wrote that "The number of our students taking Russian Soviet passports is increasing."[29] Whittemore's group specifically preferred students who still had relatives living in the U.S.S.R. They would be most motivated to participate in the ongoing "great creative Russian change."

Educators, clergy, and parents struggled to run "Sunday-Thursday" schools. (French communal schools closed on Sundays and Thursdays.) They were touted as a means to stem the powerful influences of French schools which some feared were eroding their children's sense of Russian national identity. Not all parents, it must be noted, were alarmed at this prospect. The schools promoted holiday celebrations and performances and attempted to instill reverence for the Russian heritage and Orthodoxy. They offered classes in Russian language, literature, history, geography, and singing, although the general level of instruction was mediocre and attendance sporadic.

Only about ten percent of the French population completed secondary education in this period. Although the *lycées* and *collèges* were limited in number, they provided secondary education to most Russian émigrés who took up the challenge. It usually was a challenge, in view of the required fees, aloofness of French children, and sometimes disdain of the teachers. The Russians were generally reported to be hard workers and good students; some won scholarships, but these could be withheld from non-citizens.[30] The French government agreed to set up special Russian sections in half-a dozen *lycées*, serving both boys and girls. Through these sections one could study Russian language, literature, history, and sometimes Orthodox religion.

Zemgor and a network of émigré organizations helped to sustain a few exclusively Russian schools. These ranged from a military lycée at Versailles, through boarding schools, some catering especially to orphans, to exclusive finishing schools. Such schools, both primary and secondary, were usually scrimping and scraping to get by, and they were regarded by many émigrés themselves as academically weak. The exception was the sumptuous Paris Russian Lycée, in which 200 Russian boys and girls could earn their French baccalaureates as well as study the history and geography of their own homeland. Mlle Maklakov, sister of the former Russian ambassador, had helped to found this fine institution in 1920. Lady Deterding became a patron and, with a subvention from the City of Paris, enabled the lycée to be housed in a grand Boulogne mansion. The American Red Cross gave kitchen equipment, and Pavlova was a generous donor. These substantial subsidies permitted many students to attend free of charge.

Russian émigré teachers at the secondary and university levels formed "academic groups" in twelve European countries. The group in Paris was most active, and their aims were characteristic. They were a mutual aid society in both academic and practical matters. They studied the French educational system and cooperated with French teachers. They encouraged and supported Russian students and student associations, and they promoted more profound knowledge of the Russian heritage, especially among young émigrés, but also within France generally. The Paris academic group had around eighty members.[31]

This group helped sustain a diversity of Russian schools, and one that it founded with Zemgor support, the Popular University, offered a mix of practical and traditional academic courses. These were all taught in the evening, and despite its name the Popular University was a secondary school. Young men and women who worked during the day flocked to the practical courses, in stenography, mechanical drawing, auto repair, electricity, tailoring, and embroidery. Smaller numbers studied academic subjects like French and foreign languages, music, and the piano. Twice a year, a commission, half-French and half-Russian, presided over by a

Sorbonne-appointed French professor, gave examinations for the "bac" which would allow advanced study in law or medicine. Seven or eight out of ten candidates usually passed at each session, a success rate considered more than respectable. The Popular University also offered monthly lectures on literature, art, and history that were open to the public. It organized inexpensive tours of Paris. Pierre E. Kovalevsky, one of the foremost émigré educators, has estimated that during its first ten years, the Popular University served more than 4,000 students, attracted about 9,000 to the monthly lectures, and introduced 8,000 to the cultural sites of Paris.[32]

The Popular University also established a studio of decorative art. Prince Yusupov opened a school for young artisans, and Madam Soukhotine-Tolstoy, one of Leo Tolstoy's daughters, founded a Russian Academy of Art in Paris. The Sergei Rachmaninoff Russian Conservatory taught music in the tradition of the brothers Anton and Nicholas Rubinstein, who had founded the Moscow Conservatory. The Paris school profited from its association with Rachmaninoff, enjoyed the support of wealthy patrons, and was quite successful. The ballerinas, Egorova, Kshesinskaia, Preobrazhenskaia, and Trefilova all ran flourishing schools of dance.

The Russian Higher Technical Institute developed a remarkable correspondence school with major financial support from the YMCA. There were courses in general education and in technical fields: commerce, agronomy, mechanics, electrical and civil engineering, and chemistry. Most of the technical textbooks were published in the U.S.S.R., and in the early thirties over 100 students in the Soviet Union were enrolled in the Paris-based correspondence school. More than 10,000 students in sixty-five countries were studying by correspondence in 1935.[33]

In 1925, with YMCA support, the Russian Orthodox Theological Institute was founded. Metropolitan Eulogy sponsored this seminary which became a major intellectual center of Orthodox theology. Each of the forty or so seminarians received a scholarship, but they lived in poverty, five or six together sharing rooms at the Institute. Many of them worked alongside the Cossacks as porters at the Gare de l'Est during the summer months.

The Paris Academic Group encouraged students to organize, and indeed they did. There were half-a-dozen student associations in Paris and many more throughout France and in other countries. Graduates of Moscow, St. Petersburg, and Kharkov universities maintained active alumni associations. Women with degrees organized. Students grouped themselves according to the institutions in which they were enrolled or their fields of study. These associations provided mutual aid, lectures, and many occasions for socializing.

The Russian Student Christian Movement stands out as the most dynamic of youth groups. The RSCM was closely tied to the YMCA which gave it financial support and helped it assume a truly international character. Founded in London, the YMCA held its first international congress in Paris in 1855. Its branches operated with considerable independence, supporting whichever local Christian denominations were most active, Protestant, Catholic or Orthodox. So the "Y" helped to infuse the RSCM with its apolitical, international, and ecumenical qualities, qualities hardly pleasing to the Orthodox Synod Abroad. Nicholas Klepinin, who was first on the staff of the YMCA Russian Press and then financial secretary to the Theological Institute, put it this way: "The RSCM is quite modern, progressive, in many respects, liberal in its outlook. While these characteristics lead the YMCA and other foreign friends to support it, they are exactly the characteristics less favorably received by the generally conservative Russian emigration, and particularly by the former aristocracy and people of means."[34]

Nonetheless the RSCM thrived under the vigorous leadership of outstanding figures like Berdaiev, Professor Serge Zenkovsky, a highly respected theologian first elected to chair the movement, and Mother Marie. Circles were formed in ten different countries, usually led by young adults, either clergy or laity with a serious interest in theology. The future author Zoé Oldenbourg was a member. There was study of the Bible, modern Russia and Russian religious thought, social problems in light of the gospel, and Russian literature. In addition to study sessions, there were lectures on more popular themes, concerts, and socials. The RSCM operated summer camps each year. It periodically sent out representatives to reach isolated émigrés in the provinces. Mother Marie for a time acted in that capacity. According to one of their pamphlets, "The aim of the Movement is to reawaken the latent spiritual forces in youth, to unite them with the church, to preserve the best traditions and culture, and to train leaders for future Russia."[35]

The Russian Student Christian Movement fostered the growth of the National Organization of Russian Scouts Abroad. Scouting on the Baden-Powell model had caught on quickly in pre-revolutionary Russia, and divergent émigré interests saw in scouting a means of inculcating their values. The RSCM helped revive scouting in order to teach the Christian virtues, individual moral responsibility, and respect for the Russian heritage. Those identified with the Volunteer Army supported scouting, but they emphasized respect for authority, discipline, and patriotic love of Old Russia. Generals Wrangel, Kutepov, and Miller all took a great interest in the Scout movement. These disagreements explain several breakaways from the mainstream Russian Scouts. The "Falcons" and the "Knights" emerged as separate scouting organizations. Their leaders were in the conservative and traditional mold and wished to be independent of the progressive RSCM. A line from the scout's prayer of the Knights ran, "Allow us to return soon to the Russian land."[36]

In practice these separate organizations functioned very much alike along the familiar lines of scouting. Boys and girls both participated. Scouts wore uniforms and had their special prayers, hymns, pledges, and mottos. They enjoyed physical exercise, learned practical skills, and engaged in community service. They earned merit badges. Russian Scout troops were organized in fourteen countries, including the United States, and they participated in international jamborees. Scouts went off every summer for lengthy stays in their camps.

Indeed, children's summer camps were available to most young émigrés. Every youth organization promoted the summer camp experience as a necessary part of a child's upbringing. Kovalevsky points out that Russian summer camps were especially well developed before the war. Whole train loads of Russian youth would depart in early June, leaving the Gare Lyon from which camps spread southward."[37] These camps were distinguished by the fact that the Russian flag rose over each one every morning. An Orthodox priest would usually be in attendance, the children were encouraged to speak Russian, and around the campfires Russian songs were sung. Many sports clubs maintained camps in the Alps or along the Mediterranean. Each cultural or religious organization and each parish had its own resort or children's camp. The French camps attracted Russian children from Belgium and Switzerland, even from Czechoslovakia. Under the auspices of the RSCM, some children were sent from France to England for summer language study. The same program arranged for orphans to live with Swiss families during the summers. Camp lasted from one to two months, and many thousands of young Russians thrived on the experience. In adult eyes, the camps meant more than vacation and healthy outdoor activity; they meant the teaching of desirable religious and national sentiments.

Private American philanthropic institutions played a leading role in educational support for the White émigrés in the United States. This was part of the larger American effort to encourage assimilation of the immigrant waves that had been flooding in for forty years. The Russian Student Fund was an offshoot of the Institute of International Education, and it granted loans for college and university studies. Annual individual loans ran from $400 to $500. The Fund was geared to those pursuing practical subjects, most often engineering, rather than purely academic ones. And in the early years the Fund directors expected its beneficiaries to return to the U.S.S.R. In 1925 an observer commented that "Funds are being advanced to students with the understanding that they will actively participate in Russia's work of reconstruction and eventually return the amounts advanced."[38] White refugees themselves agreed with this assessment, looking forward with their confreres in Europe to the eventual return.

The New York Times carried several stories on the Russian Student Fund and dramatized the backgrounds of aid recipients: "A son of a regimental priest, now studying under the fund at Johns Hopkins University, eked out a living for a time in a garage in Egypt, where labor gets a low wage. Later he sweltered for eight months in the boiler room of a cotton mill in Egypt to earn his passage money to America. Another hunted seals in the Arctic until his ship was sunk by a German submarine; then he took to gold hunting, fish peddling, automobile washing, and the selling of women's stockings in China, Japan, Spain and France, until he had money enough to come to America. A Russian student of farming at the University of Vermont has supported himself by working first in a blacksmith shop, then in a machine shop, and then as a teacher and choirmaster in a Russian church."[39] Fund policy was to spread the wealth among as many different institutions as possible. By 1945 the Fund had lent over $600,000 to 650 students enrolled in 106 different colleges and universities.[40] Only a few women were included, perhaps five percent of the total. Reversing this ratio and offering traditional academic studies, Catholic educators sponsored "young Russian men and women who are unable to carry on their studies under the Soviet regime." Fifteen Catholic institutions reserved twenty-nine scholarships for Russian men, and twenty-two institutions specified fifty-three scholarships for Russian women.[41]

American public schools, particularly in large immigration centers like New York City, held free evening classes in English, and sometimes there were lessons in "citizenship" and basic job skills. The YMCA scheduled English classes, for modest fees, at convenient times during the day and evening. The local "Y" helped a significant number of immigrants find their bearings in the new world.

Out of the YWCA had come the International Institute movement, beginning in 1911. Its initial purpose was to teach English to young immigrant women and to aid them in finding jobs and housing. Edith Terry Bremer, a veteran of the University of Chicago Settlement, founded the International Institutes on the settlement house model. She rejected "Americanization" and believed that immigrants should prize their ethnic heritage. She laid down the novel policy of staffing the Institutes with educated young women from the appropriate ethnic groups. The Institutes became, as Bremer said, "possessed by the people they serve."[42] Most Institutes were independent of the YWCA in the 1930s. Their function broadened from protecting the immigrant girl to concern for the family and community, thus for men and women, young and old.

The New York International Institute maintained six different ethnic centers, one especially for Russians. It continued to lay stress on the teaching of English and offered classes in other languages as well. English lessons were free as was general counseling. The Advisory Service Department helped people with questions about naturalization and citizenship. Kyra Malkokvsky received special recognition for her work with the White émigrés. She herself came over in 1917 with Ambassador Bakhmeteff's entourage. As an employee of the International Institute, she advised many of her compatriots and often acted as their witness for naturalization.[43]

The New York Institute developed a broad educational program somewhat along the lines of the Popular University in Paris. There were classes in cooking, homemaking, dance, drama, singing, and crafts. In 1939, the Russian Children's Group in Folk Arts instructed 617 young people. There were excursions to see the cultural sites of the city. Lectures and discussions explored American life. An Employment Department endeavored to place both men and women in jobs. The yearly membership dues were $1, and that allowed entrée to many social events in the 17th Street residence building: holiday parties, dances, drama workshops and fireside discussions. This building included an auditorium, club rooms, a gymnasium, cafeteria, and two residence floors for women.[44] Edith Terry Bremer's vision resulted in an agency that effectively reinforced the self-confidence of immigrants. Russian refugees in New York could attest to that.

A number of Russian vocational and technical schools, some short-lived, were launched in the United States during the interwar period. The most successful, and the one most relevant to White émigrés, was the Russian Collegiate Institute in New York City. Seed money of $10,000 came from the Carnegie Fund in 1918. The New York Board of Education provided classrooms, and with additional Carnegie grants and tuition the Institute was able to keep going. Alexander Petrunkevitch, an eminent zoologist and professor at Yale, lent his prestige to the Institute as its president.

The Institute was set up to serve working people with classes in the evenings and on weekends. There were three departments: preparatory, academic, and technical. The preparatory program required study of English along with a series of basic courses taught in Russian: geography, history, math, and science. Petrunkevitch explained this regimen as preparation for entrance to "places like Cooper Union."[45] The academic department offered broader educational courses on weekends and brought in eminent lecturers such as Igor Sikorsky and the renowned Russian historian Paul Vinogradov. The technical department worked in conjunction with the YMCA, and its typical classes were in shop math, mechanical drawing, agriculture, and applied biology. Lecturers from the Russian Collegiate Institute frequently spoke before Russian organizations in a number of cities. Public lectures were popular. With its mixed curriculum of practical and academic subjects and its public lectures program the Russian Collegiate Institute resembled, on a far more modest scale, the Popular University in Paris. In another parallel to the European scene, Petrunkevitch was president of a New York "academic group."

The Orthodox Church in America had established a network of parish schools well before the White émigrés appeared. According to the Census Bureau in 1916 there were 126 parish schools with 6,739 pupils.[46] English and Russian and religion were taught evenings and weekends and during summers. The parishes also supported adult and children's theatrical groups which were popular community institutions. The Orthodox parish schools were reorganized in the middle thirties on the model of the American Sunday school. The Church maintained a scholarship fund for college students and seminarians. The St. Vladimir's Seminary opened in Manhattan in 1938 and became a leading center for the study of Orthodox theology.[47] These church schools, of course, primarily served the children of the pre-revolutionary immigrants, and the trend was that fewer and fewer children studied the Russian language.

Russian lay schools in the United States were also largely the preserve of the old immigration. The New York Federation of Russian Grammar Schools ordered 300 textbooks from the Soviet Union in 1926, hardly material that would appeal to the Whites.[48] ROOVA founded a Saturday school near its Lakewood, NJ cooperative farm where over 100 children studied Russian language and literature, geography, and history. In the late thirties, parents became increasingly alarmed that their children were losing the ancestral language (actively rejecting it in fact). They petitioned city and state governments to include Russian in the public school curriculum, but to no avail.

Youth organizations in some cases bridged Europe and America. The Russian Student Christian Movement, facilitated by its YMCA connection, involved some young people in the United States. There were a few Russian Scout and Falcon troops which offered possibilities of summer camping. ROOVA's Lakewood community maintained a children's summer camp featuring Russian language lessons. The extensive grounds were made up of a wooded park for picnicking, pine woods for gathering nuts and mushrooms, a lake for swimming and fishing, and tennis courts. In 1926, a Federation of Russian Orthodox Clubs ("R" clubs) was formed. Over the next ten years it expanded into 100 chapters with 2,500 members. The clubs engaged in a variety of cultural, religious, athletic, and charitable activities.[49] Most children who participated in these groups were American-born. Far fewer White émigré children were to be found in the United States than in Europe.

SUMMARY

Russian refugee organizations proliferated during the interwar period. A Russian Committee of United Organizations was set up in Paris to facilitate cooperation among those groups worldwide that had more than purely local interests. In 1924 there were sixty-seven member organizations; in 1929 there were 175; and by 1936 there were 325 such organizations.[50] If one were to count the unaffiliated social and cultural groups, the numbers would multiply many times over. Sheer survival for the refugees was precarious. They legitimately felt vulnerable, and this was the cause of their penchant for formal organization. Joined together they could at best protect themselves and at least provide one another mutual aid and comfort.

The impulse to help those most in need was the single most pervasive theme tying these organizations together. The Volunteer Army veteran organizations, Zemgor, and the Russian Red Cross were typically engaged in fund raising, both inside and outside the exile community, for their particular constituencies.

The exile community in the United States appeared in a number of ways to be a miniature of the one in France. Both groups faced hardships and counted on remarkably parallel and sometimes identical organizations to carry them through. Both groups were active on behalf of the worldwide Russian emigration. Both were solicitous about the fate of their children and struggled with the inexorable denationalization of the younger generation. Both showed great concern for education and in face of increasing discouragement dreamed of the eventual return to Mother Russia. Both the French and American emigrations were fractured politically as exemplified by divisions in the Church and the émigré press.

The relatively small group of White Russians in the United States felt their isolation, whereas those in France were conscious of being the center of Russia Abroad. The great weight of the old immigration in the United States, with its networks of churches and mutual aid organizations, gave the White newcomers some foundation to build on but also burdened them with strained relations, an uneasy liaison with people of very different social roots and values. The refugees in Europe received substantial aid from governments and international organizations like the League of Nations and the Red Cross. Private philanthropic institutions played a more important role in the United States, e.g., the Russian Student Fund, the Carnegie Fund, the International Institutes. Monies tended increasingly to flow from America to Europe. Wealthy Americans made generous contributions through such organizations as the Red Cross and Whittemore's Education Committee. Émigrés in the United States extended aid overseas by means of their own societies, like the Literary Fund and the Emigrant Children's Welfare Society. They were quicker to naturalize in the United States than elsewhere. The time and energy that many émigrés spent in their organizations reveal an extraordinary commitment to helping. They strained mightily, and for the few they made success and contentment possible; for the many they were able to ameliorate despair with a few rays of hope.

NOTES TO CHAPTER 6

1. Pierre E. Kovalevsky, *Zarubezhnaia Rossiia; istoriia i kul'turnoprosvetitel'naia rabota russkogo zarubezh'ia za polveka (Emigré Russia; History and the Cultural-Educational Work*

of Russia Abroad for Half a Century), 1920-1970 (Paris, 1971), 332-333.

2. This observation made by Tatiana Aleksinskaia, "Russkaia emigratsia (Russian Emigration) 1920-1939," *Vozrozhdenie (Renaissance)* (Paris post-war journal), No. 60 (Dec. 1956), 37.

3. *Rousski Invalide*, No. 129 Apri. 5, 1939, 7 & No. 134, June 20, 1939, 6. (Organ of the Russian Disabled Veterans Association, published in Paris.)

4. A. Kartashev, *Russkii nasional'nyi soiuz (Russian National Associaton)* (Collection of the Russian National Committee) (Paris, 1936), 46.

5. John J. Stephan, *The Russian Fascists — Tragedy and Farce in Exile, 1925-1945* (New York, 1978), 217.

6. *Aperçu de l'activité du Comité (des Zemstvos et Villes)* (Fev. 1921-Avril 1922 (Paris, 1922), 19, Vserossiiskii zemskii soiuz, Box 9, Bakhmeteff Archive, Columbia University.

7. Vadim V. Rudnev, *The Educational Work of the Russian Zemstvos and Towns Relief Committee Abroad* (Paris, 1927), 11-12.

8. *Zemgor budget for 1926 (France)*, Association pour la conservation des valeurs culturelles russes, 1917-1947, 8 AS, 138, Archives nationales, Paris.

9. *Russkii Krasnyi Krest' posle 1917 goda . . . (The Russian Red Cross after 1917)* (Paris, ca. 1926), 36.

10. Charles Ledré, *Les émigrés russes en France* (Paris, 1930), 126.

11. *La Croix Rouge russe — aperçu de l'activité pour l'année 1935*, pp. 5-6, M.M. Fedorov, Box 17, Bakhmeteff Archive, Columbia University.

12. *The Red Cross Courier*, Vol. 17, No. 10 (Apr. 1938), 26.

13. *Russkoe trudovoe khristianskoe dvizhenie*, Khoromanskii, single folder, Bakhmeteff Archive, Columbia University.

14. Jean Delage, *La Russie en exil* (Paris, 1930), 36-37.

15. Taya Zinkin, *Odious Child* (London, 1971), 88.

16. Ibid., 103-104.

17. Editors of ROOVA's newsletter referred to themselves as "sons of peasants." *Russkii vestnik (Russian Herald)*, No. 60 (May 1, 1937), 19.

18. *Desiat' let zhizni ROOVA (ROOVA's First Ten Years), 1926-1936* (New York, 1936), 151.

19. Katharine Strelsky, "Alexandra Lvovna Tolstoy (1 July 1884-26 September 1979)," *Russian Review*, 39 No. 4 (Oct. 1980): 530.

20. Y. J. Chyz and J. S. Roucek, "The Russians in the United States," *Slavonic Review*. 17, No. 51 (Apr. 1939): 652.

21. *Obshchestvo Pomoshchi Russkim Detiam za Rubezhom, 1926-1951: kratkii istoricheskii ocherk deiatel'nosti obshestvo (The Russian Emigrant Children's Welfare Society, 1926-1951: An Historical Overview of its Activity)* (New York, 1951), 14.

22. *Zarubezhnaia russkaia shkola (The Russian School Abroad)*, 1920-1924 (Paris, 1924), 3-5.

23. *The Children of Russian Refugees in Western Europe* (Paris, ca. 1928), 7.

24. Ibid., 20.

25. *Deiatel'nost' tsentral'nago komiteta (Activity of the Central Committee), 1922-23 to 1931-32*, pp. 57-58, M.M. Fedorov, Box 11, Bakhmeteff Archive, Columbia University.

26. M.M. Fedorov, Box 10, 11, 17, Bakhmeteff Archive, Columbia University.

27. Ledré, 118-120.

28. *Letter from Seth T. Gano, Treasurer, to S. Rachmaninoff, Jan. 6, 1930*, Committee for the Education of Russian Youth in Exile, Box 1, Bakhmeteff Archive, Columbia University.

29. *Report of Director, 1925-1926*, Committee for the Education of Russian Youth in

Exile, Box 24, Bakhmeteff Archive, Columbia University.

30. Tatiana Metternich, *Purgatory of Fools* (New York, 1976), 38.

31. G. de Reynold, *Les groupes académiques russes* (Geneva, L. of N. Report, 1923), 7-9.

32. Kovalevsky, 90.

33. W. Chapin Huntington, *The Homesick Million, Russia-out-of-Russia* (Boston, 1933), pp. 126-128. Aleksinskaia, "Emigratsiia i ee molodoe pokolenie (The Emigration and its Younger Generation)," *Vozrozhdenie*, No. 65 (May 1957), 34-35.

34. *YMCA. Survey of the North American YMCA Service to Russians in Europe, 1930*, p. 135, Foreign — Russians in Europe, YWCA, National Board Archives, N.Y.

35. *Russia's Youth Abroad*, ca. 1928, Association pour la conservation des valeurs culturelles russes, 1917-1947, 8 AS, 101, Archives nationales, Paris.

36. *Organisation nationale vitiaz* (Paris, 1960), 3.

37. Kovalevsky, 66.

38. "Russian Students in American Colleges," *The Interpreter*, 4, No. 9 (Nov. 1925): 16.

39. "Russian Students' Fund Aids Refugees to Gain Schooling," *New York Times*, (Dec. 27, 1925), viii, 6.

40. Alexis R. Wiren, "The Russian Student Fund, 1920-1945," *Russian Review*, 5, No. 1 (Autumn 1945): 104-110.

41. *New York Times*, (April 17, 1927), 3.

42. *Spectrum*, III, No. 1 (May 1977) (University of Minnesota Immigration Research Center), 2.

43. "Letter from Florence G. Cassidy, Chm., Admin., Comt., Nat'l Council on Naturalization and Citizenship, to Thomas S. Griffing, District Director, U.S. Naturalization Bureau, NYC (May 29, 1933), E30-830, Dist. 3 (NY), Citizenship Education File, Records of the Immigration and Naturalization Service, RG 85, National Archives.

44. *The International Institute in 1939* (New York, annual report), Box 65, International Institute, YWCA, National Board Archives, New York.

45. A. Petrunkevitch, "The Russian Problem in the United States," *The Standard*, 6 (Feb. 1920): 178.

46. Gennady Klimenko, "Russians in New Jersey," in Barbara Cunningham (ed.) *The New Jersey Ethnic Experience* (Union City, NJ, 1977), 384.

47. Paul R. Magocsi, "Russians," *Harvard Encyc. of Amer. Ethnic Groups* (Cambridge, Ma, 1980), 890.

48. *Novyi mir (New World)*, (Oct. 16, 1926), 15.

49. Klimenko, 387.

50. Kovalevsky, 24-25.

VII. Between Two Worlds

Complete assimilation of the White émigrés into their host societies would have meant a loss of their sense of Russian "peoplehood." The totally assimilated, following Milton Gordon's analysis, would adopt the cultural patterns of the new country. They would freely enter into cliques, clubs, and institutions of the host society on the primary group level of intimate relationships. There would be large-scale intermarriage between immigrants and natives. The assimilated would not encounter prejudice or discrimination; neither would they experience value or power conflict.[1]

First-generation immigrants do not assimilate. What happens is partly the result of the newcomers' behavior and partly the result of the settled population's responses. A term recently preferred to describe this interaction is "integration," which suggests that immigrants make a series of adjustments, but that they affect the dominant society itself, and that all parties change through time.[2] The question is one of degree. To what extent did the Russian refugees successfully adjust to their new environment; to what extent did they remain alienated? The answers are highly individualized and depend on a great number of variables.

The first and foremost variable in determining an individual's fate is her or his class. This has become a truism in the field of immigration studies. Occupation, wealth, and education are of utmost importance in understanding why some immigrants have been well integrated and others have not. In the United States, persistent ethnic pride has been characteristic of the working class.[3] The upwardly mobile tend to be less conscious of an apartness from society as a whole. A study of Italian and Polish immigrants into France found class distinctions to be most significant in explaining individual propensities to integrate or to remain segregated: "The most radical differences do not seem to be due as much to the nationality of immigrants as to the economic and social milieu in which they evolve and to which they belong."[4] The history of American immigration shows that rates of naturalization have not varied with nationality, but rather with socio-cultural differences: "Those newcomers with higher educational, occupational and income levels tend to become citizens soonest."[5]

Those of higher class, though, do not always integrate the most easily. The large contingent of upper-class White émigrés was extremely anxious to preserve class distinctions exactly as they had existed "before the deluge," and within the exile community these subtle levels of status were maintained with remarkable success. But one's past status was no guarantee of integration into the adopted society. The aristocrat who became a Renault assembly line worker suffered status degradation, and his sense of alienation from the French was accordingly intensified. The bulk of White émigrés found themselves sharply downgraded in their new countries. Their sensitivity to past glories made their subsequent situation all the more difficult to accept. At every socioeconomic level, the individuals who were able to move horizontally within a given class (or to rise) were the ones who could most easily integrate.

Former peasants and cossacks that worked French land for several years usually adjusted well. Albert Thomas, who facilitated the influx of contracted labor into France during the 1920s, noted this and believed that rural life encouraged assimilation more than did urban.[6] He had a point, for the Cossack who successfully farmed in France earned the respect of his peasant neighbors and felt a corresponding sense of ease in his new milieu. Urban and rural distinctions were emphasized by Mlle Madeleine Doré in her 1947 survey of Russian immigrants. She found aristocrats and intellectuals still concentrated in Paris, whereas peasants, workers, and the middle class were dispersed in the provinces and better assimilated. Doré observed a greater propensity among workers and rural folk for mixed marriage and saw that as speeding their assimilation.[7] Separation from one's own ethnic group almost always forces a faster pace of adjustment to a new society. This path was consciously taken by the young Anatole Mazour, later to be an eminent historian of Russia. Upon his arrival in the United States in 1922, he was advised by a Columbia University professor to break with the New York émigré colony in order to master English and American ways more rapidly. Mazour accordingly went west to pursue his academic studies and felt that the experience profited him well.[8]

Residence in an ethnic enclave generally hinders a sense of identification with the host society, but this womb-like protection may give an individual the strength eventually to cut the umbilical cord with his motherland. The Russian refugees that are our concern typically lived in "Little Russias" with their strong social, religious, and commercial bonds. The ambivalence of the hosts mandates such clustering: "The majority community allows the immigrant to come in, but it treats him with reserve and suspicion....The immigrant tends to respond to the new environment with a combination of adjustment to the wider community and simultaneous withdrawal into a partially separate group within it. The ethnic community is a semi-withdrawn subcommunity."[9] As long as the drive for security was paramount, individuals preferred close-knit ties with their ethnic group. In time, as the urge for material advancement was reasserted, they were increasingly willing to risk contacts with the outside world. Ethnic enclaves have been made up of the three basic elements of traditional society: family, church, and local community. As the modern values of independence, secularism, and mobility have eroded traditional institutions, more individuals have been able to join the ranks of the larger society.[10]

The younger the immigrant, the greater the likelihood of his feeling at home in the adopted country. Those who had left Russia as adults carried that ethnic imprint with them the rest of their lives. But by the late 1920s parents were beginning to complain that their children were losing Russian nationality and acquiring French or American ones. The Grand Duchess Marie observed that young people, in 1932, still felt themselves to be Russian but that they were not interested in the old quarrels which so animated their parents. They were free of preconceptions, lived in the present, and were prepared to go forward. Zoé Oldenbourg was one of those young people. She was nine years of age when she left Russia for Paris in 1925. Her experience corroborates Marie's opinion. Oldenbourg, active in the Student Christian Movement, found her contemporaries to be less concerned with politics than their elders. They became impatient with their parents' repeated assertion that "Russia will need you." Oldenbourg also notes that the émigré children ten years younger than she (typically born in France) tended to speak French among themselves and to forget Russian.[11] It would be very difficult to live in France, however, and be oblivious to politics. Many Russian youth, although feeling less intensely than their parents, were drawn to the right, and that at least was a link between the generations. But the smaller number who embraced ecumenical Christianity or who were attracted to the ideals of socialism or Marxism gave the older generation much cause to complain.

K. Partchevsky in a 1937 article about Russian exiles in France distinguished three groups. The children born in France were attending French schools and readily adapting to their environment. Parental influence was limited by the need of both parents to work. So the children spoke Russian badly and usually could not read or write it. The youth of university age were ambivalent. Some proudly disdained naturalization. Some desired naturalization but were thwarted by official discouragement and restrictions. Adults by and large could not make a satisfying life for themselves in France. "The condition of the adults and of the older youth can currently be considered tragic," concluded Partchevsky.[12] For him, the émigrés overall were exhausted and passive.

Vladimir Varshavskii referred to the "unseen generation" in describing those who left Russia in adolescence. They felt themselves to be in limbo, living apart from the world and from history. They had no clear-cut responsibilities and no well-defined sense of self. "Of all 'superfluous men' of the Russian past and of all the 'lost generations' of Europe and America they considered themselves the most 'superfluous' and the most 'lost.'"[13] Their parents were ill at ease in emigration but had formerly exercised meaningful responsibilities. The older generation retained their memories of accomplishments and of place and purpose in life. The young people had been groomed for a way of life which they in no part could ever realize. Hence the particular bitterness of their exile.

Two post-World War II French studies presented evidence that the

Russian émigrés were maintaining their sense of exclusivity. The youth were commonly upwardly mobile, and three-quarters of those in higher education were enrolled in scientific programs, a career in science being valued for its professional status as well as material rewards. But the Russians still tended to live in communities clustered arou⟨n⟩d their churches. Social or professional contacts with the French were uncommon; the exceptions were Russian artists and scientists who belonged to French associations. Most Russians expressed resentment at what they perceived to be official discrimination and inconsistency toward them. Russians had a greater number of non-naturalized children than the Armenian immigrants with whom they were being compared. And even naturalization did not mean that an émigré had lost his or her Russian spirit.[14] Another survey also remarked on the aspiration of young émigrés, their hard work at school, their parents' willingness to sacrifice, and the generally successful adaptation of those who were able to complete their education in France. On the other hand, higher class Russians were described as usually "déclassé," feeling keenly the affront of living among French people less cultivated than themselves. The children of the Clamart Russian enclave appeared to be not all assimilated, an anomaly attributed to their very aristocratic origins and their education in private schools.[15]

"In Europe Russians feel themselves less torn from Russia, but in America, separated from Europe by an ocean, with the slowness even of postal communication, Russians all felt themselves to be deeply cut off from Russia, as if thrown forever into strange circumstances, a foreign world to which they had to adjust."[16] This was the conclusion of Vasilii Zen'kovskii who spent nine months of 1926 in the United States under the auspices of the Russian Student Christian Movement. It was his gloomy impression that most Russian immigrants embraced the external qualities of American life, e.g., the pragmatism, the fascination with technology, the pursuit of money. He lamented the lack of spirituality, the self-centeredness, and among the youth, the ignorance of Russian, frivolity, and degree of Americanization. One's assessment need not be so negative, but there is no question that young White refugees integrated more rapidly into American society than into French. Argus has pointed to one cause by noting that the intelligentsia had no access to special schools in the United States; consequently, their children spoke no Russian.[17]

The importance of language skill in adapting to a new society is fundamental. Until very recently in the United States, prevailing values and the public school system gave no support to the retention of non-English languages. This widened the gulf between immigrants and their American-born children but hastened the process of integration. One aspect of successful adjustment was the achievement of professional status, and that almost always required a very good knowledge of the host language.

Individual members of the large, self-contained Russian enclaves in France could get by without learning French. In their 1946 study of the Paris region, Robert Gessain and Madeleine Doré determined that one-third of the older White émigrés spoke French badly or not at all. Obviously, this kept them isolated from their adopted society.

Russian women on the whole appear to have more successfully adapted to exile life than did the men. The case of the White refugees supports the recent hypothesis of M. Estellie Smith who "questions the accepted wisdom that males and children acculturate more quickly to the new environment than do wives and mothers. The women studied had to adopt to a whole spectrum of new ways with respect to shopping, schooling for their children, neighborhood geography, public transportation, and relations with the people around them. They were also expected by their families to maintain certain old ways....This pressure for selective marginality, writes Smith, required a high degree of adaptation, but it was adaptation of a special kind."[18]

A striking example of the woman's taking charge is offered by Marie Balascheff in her autobiography, *The Transplanting*. Balascheff's background was one of aristocratic refinement and luxury; she had lived for several years in Washington, D.C., when her father was ambassador there. Being reduced to exile in France, however, she purchased rundown land on the Picardy coast. Over several years of unremitting, hard physical labor, she, her three sons, and a nephew developed into successful poultry farmers. Meanwhile her husband, a former marshal of the nobility, remained in Paris and no longer functioned as a member of the family. He rates barely a mention in Balascheff's narrative. The experience of the Grand Duchess Marie was comparable. For a time her husband helped manage her embroidery business, but he lost interest, they drifted apart, and eventually separated. Tatiana Metternich felt that the revolution had been more devastating to men than women. She believed that her mother coped better in exile than her father because of her orientation to family and friends. "For women, the collapse of man-made laws holding the framework of Government together was perhaps less of a personal failure. Much more than institutions, Mamma regretted people, things, the country, and above all, Petersburg!"[19] Marguerite Cassini (mother of designer Oleg Cassini) echoes these sentiments in describing her husband's life in Washington, D.C: "Sacha adores America, its iceboxes, its comforts, everything; but he still lives and talks in Russian. At the Ambassador (Hotel) he meets daily a small Russian colony and that is his world. There he can talk of the past, of the mistakes of the Tsar, of the grandeur of his country, of the uniforms, of the decorations, of the changes of government and life in the past, always in the past."[20] Since traditionally a man's work has been primary to his self-definition, it is not surprising that his loss of it would be traumatic. Few of the women in the White wave of émigrés were wedded to careers.

Intermarriage of immigrant and host is prima facie evidence of integration. Both the émigrés and French observers agreed that mixed marriages were numerous among workers and provincials, whereas they were rare for the middle class and intellectuals. In France where there were two or three male émigrés for each female, Russian men married Frenchwomen much more frequently than Russian women married Frenchmen. Mlle Doré calculated in her study that mixed marriages had averaged more than 3,000 a year in France during the 1930s, a surprisingly high number given the overall impression of the isolation of the Russian community. But we have focused on the refugees concentrated in Paris, precisely the ones of such class and education as to be least likely to intermarry. Doré asserts that "When the mother is French, the children are French." Such children were usually raised as Catholic which effectively divorced them from a very important part of the Russian experience.[21] Serge Rubakine, who spent his adult life as a laborer in France, married a Bretonne with whom he had three children. He spoke Russian to them as children, and they understood but always replied in French. When interviewed in the 1970s, Rubakine blithely pronounced his children to be ninety-eight percent French.[22]

Even though their children absorbed French culture, the Frenchwomen who married émigrés often made their own adjustments to the Russian way of life and entered to some degree into the Russian colony. Doré and other have noted this tendency. The Russian women who did marry Frenchmen usually maintained contacts with the émigré community, exemplifying the strong pull of the Russian milieu for all those who initially belonged to it.

Journalist Michael Argus caused a stir within the New York White Russian colony when he married an Anglo-Saxon American woman. Such liaisons outside the group were exceptional. As Argus wryly observed, marriage to an American "was a perfidious betrayal of Russian émigré womanhood, of all the widows, divorcées, and spinsters who had lost another eligible male to the enemy camp."[23] Argus also describes the constant efforts of his fellow émigrés to draw his wife into their culture, a process she spiritedly resisted but not with complete success.

It has been characteristic of immigrants into the United States to marry within a common religious heritage even after they began to cross ethnic lines. Ruby Jo Reeves Kennedy first postulated this "triple melting pot theory" in 1944 which holds that Americans tend to marry within the three overall categories of Protestant, Catholic, or Jewish. Since their religious affiliation had become a newly important source of identification of them in exile, the Russian émigrés were drawn to follow this pattern, Orthodox marrying Orthodox, and that of course worked to sustain the group's sense of apartness from mainstream American society.

Refugees who deliberately chose to settle in either the United States or France, however, seldom did so with marriage in mind. France offered political opportunities and cultural attractions for many intellectuals. Political activists naturally gravitated to Paris, headquarters of every émigré political movement from left to right. The exile community's political leaders and major spokesmen were in Paris, so that city was a magnet to refugees worldwide. Paris air was free. French passion for politics, the ferment of ideas, the liberty to speak out were enthralling to those who had suffered tsarist or Bolshevik repression. France was a Great Power and its people, a cosmopolitan society, thus a suitable arena from which fervent exiles could declaim their tragedy. Nina Berberova has summed up the cultural attractions of France: the strong infusion of French language and thought into Russian culture; the memories of forebears who had found a second home in France; the acceptable ideas that children brought home from their French schools.[24] One could still feel connections to old Russia while living in France.

Public life in France was appealing, but private life was usually onerous for émigrés, and on that level they found it difficult to integrate. Restrictions on working rights, expulsion orders, the seeming caprice of government authorities, all kept Russians in an agitated state. Most émigrés lived in poverty and thus were cut off from the body of society. As Zoé Oldenbourg explained, "the French" for the typical refugee were the concierge who demanded to be paid four times a year, the feared gas and electric worker who would cut off power for non-payment, and the grocer to whom one was in debt and who might withdraw credit.[25]

The Russian and French ways of life clashed in numerous cultural dissonances. Russians were stymied by French reserve and closed family life, complaining of French "coldness" and reluctance to invite guests into their homes. French individualism seemed selfish, concern for order and economy appeared petty, thrift was denounced as miserliness. In contrast to Russian boisterousness, openness, and prodigality, the French were aware of limits and were somewhat world-weary and skeptical. They desired measure in all things and a careful delineation of roles and observance of social rules. The politeness and gallantry of the French struck émigrés as superficial. Russians indulged their enthusiasms; the French had a knowing air that everything has already been thought, said, and done. The opportunities for misunderstandings were rife on both sides.

Widely held French stereotypes of the White emigration were decidedly negative. The Whites were thought to be reactionary, supporters of tsarist despotism and repressors of the peasant masses. If not that, they were irresponsible dupes who had passively submitted to the odious Bolshevik regime. They were the vanquished, those who did not work, those "who eat our bread." It was not easy.

Immigrants into the United States enjoyed a more secure legal status than did refugees in France or most other countries. Government regulations were less obtrusive, legal restrictions less oppressive. The White

Russian in the United States need not register with the police nor carry an identity card. He or she was positively encouraged to naturalize which made him or her feel more welcome than in France. And since Americans were a multitude of ethnic groups, attaining U.S. citizenship did not imply a renouncing of one's ethnicity. By the late twenties a White émigré who applied for U.S. citizenship would likely be commended by his fellows, contrary to the case in France.[26] The United States was remote from Russia, and this allowed a psychological distancing of the exiles from their homeland which made integration into American society easier.

Multinational immigration into the United States was a well-established phenomenon, and agencies like the public schools and International Institutes were in place to facilitate adjustment of newcomers. After the Red Scare peaked in 1921, the official stance that all citizens must be one hundred percent American and wipe out their pasts began to soften. In 1924 Horace Kallen introduced the term "cultural pluralism," the conception that a healthy society could consist of diverse groups who remained conscious and proud of their distinct heritages. Although deep-seated popular prejudices toward foreigners persisted, subsequent changes slowly worked to make America more accommodating to her ethnic minorities, including the Russians. As summarized by Richard Weiss: "The increased power of ethnics and the drive to unify the country against fascism called forth a new set of cultural imperatives. Diversity became legitimate, even desirable. Prejudice and intolerance became pathologies to be studied and cured. Minorities acquired cultural rights in addition to legal ones."[27]

More U.S. citizens were active Communists or Communist sympathizers during the Depression years than before or after. Overall, however, communism seemed more antithetical to American society than to French, and that gave a modicum of comfort to the White Russians here. Russian aristocrats, genuine and bogus, were the objects of particular adulation on the part of a good many Americans. Wealthy Americans tended to be more straightforwardly sympathetic with the White expatriates than were their French counterparts. The relatively free and easy ways of Americans were more appealing to émigrés as a rule than the French reserve.

The American way of life, though, also held its frustrations for the White Russian immigrants. Although the remoteness of the United States from Russia could cause dreams of the old country to fade more quickly, it meant that the new land was unconnected, strange, and took a good deal of getting used to. The free and easy manners had their appeal but could also appear too amorphous and superficial. Russians, as have other immigrants, frequently complained that the United States lacked traditions, it changed too fast, that it was anti-intellectual and provincial. Besides that, its food was bland. Americans were barbarians, unappreciative of literature, the arts, culture in general. The popular slogan to "keep smiling" could not dislodge the Russian taste for melancholy and *Weltschmerz*. American individualism was no more welcome than French. Americans often seemed crass in their material pursuits and obsession with time and punctuality. Argus explained. "To Russians time means nothing....One is wealthy when one has plenty of time on his hands." He also pointed to another cultural difference: "We [Russians] always say what we think; they [Americans] always think what to say."[28] Considerable prejudice and stereotyping are evident in these charges, but it all helps to explain the halting steps toward integration.

There is no doubt that the larger body of White refugees who settled in France retained their sense of exclusivity longer than their counterparts in the United States. Pre-revolutionary Russian art and culture were better known and appreciated in France which helped to feed the national pride of the exile colony there. The impact of the Ballets Russes, of Bakst, Benois, Goncharova, and Stravinsky had been profound. To be Orthodox in Catholic France was to stand apart. To be Orthodox in the United States was simply to be one more in a great variety of religious denominations. When Pierre Kovalevsky surveyed the scene in 1971, he likened the Russians in France to French-Canadians. He believed that the former were "denationalized" in that they had become accustomed to French institutions and were loyal French citizens. But Kovalevsky maintained that they had not lost their national character and were not like the local inhabitants. They regained their pride in world-renowned Russian culture and in the Russian language.[29]

Integration in the United States was certainly faster but not complete. In both countries, parents have commonly given their children Russian names. And adherence to the Russian Orthodox Church is the rule. Successive waves of Russian refugees to the United States may have prolonged the process of integration. The Whites were followed by displaced persons after World War II. Some earlier immigrants exerted themselves to help the newcomers and were thus exposed afresh to Russian language and culture.[30]

Ultimately, what is most striking about the original generation of White refugees is the powerful nostalgia that they felt for the Motherland. Again and again there are references to "the return." Paul Magocsi's summary of émigré literature sees it "dominated by three themes: a nationalistic love for the motherland; the difficulty of becoming accustomed to foreign ways; and loneliness."[31] The very social structure of the emigration remained firmly anchored in pre-revolutionary Russia. How many conversations turned on the past, the past where one had felt truly at home for the last time—in Moscow or Petersburg or a country estate. The revolution was endlessly replayed. What had been the point of no return? Who was to blame? The last words on these haunting visions of old Russia belong to one who grew up with them:

The children almost wanted to return in order to see the shades of these uncles, aunts and grandfathers who ceaselessly loomed behind them, floating somewhere between earth and sky in a land of legends, both somber and luminous.

A country which is there and which is not there, of which one speaks always as if it were the sole truth—as if one had left it only yesterday—a country to which no one can return, the eternal "over there." A country where one could gather mushrooms by the basketfull, where all the windows were doublepaned, where one used to go boating on the lakes—where one attended the theater and political meetings, and where the snow did not melt from November to March.[32]

NOTES TO CHAPTER VII

1. Milton Gordon, *Human Nature, Class, and Ethnicity* (Oxford, 1978), 169.

2. Julie Pycior, "Acculturation and Pluralism in Recent Studies of American Immigration History," *Ethnic and Immigration Groups: The United States, Canada, and England*, eds. Patricia J.F. Rosof et al. (New York, 1983), 25.

3. Stephen Steinberg, *The Ethnic Myth: Race, Ethnicity, and Class in America* (New York, 1981), 53-54.

4. Girard and Stoetzel, *Français et immigrés* (Paris, 1954), 99.

5. William S. Bernard, "The Integration of Immigrants in the United States," *International Migration Review*, 1 (Spring 1967): 30-31.

6. Marcel Paon, *L'immigration en France* (Paris, 1926), 13.

7. Mlle Madeleine Doré, "Enquête sur l'immigration russe," *Documents sur l'immigration*, eds. Louis Chevalier et al. (Paris, 1947), 141-147.

8. Wayne S. Vucinich, Mazour's obituary in the *Russian Review*, 41 (July 1982): 362.

9. Alex Simirenko, *Pilgrims, Colonists, and Frontiersmen* (New York, 1964), ix.

10. Steinberg, 57.

11. Zoé Oldenbourg, *Visages d'un autoportrait* (Paris,1976), 222.

12. K. Partchevsky, "Dans l'emigration-statisque generale et situation legale des émigrés en France," *Russie et chrétienté*, 1(Jan.-Mar. 1937): 106-107.

13. Vladimir Varshavskii, *Nezamechennoe pokolenie (The Unseen Generation)* (New York, 1956), 9. The "superfluous man" is a perennial character of nineteenth-century Russian literature.

14. Robert Gessain and Madeleine Doré, "Facteurs comparés d'assimilation chez des Russes et des Arméniens," *Population*, 1 (Jan. 1946): 103-108.

15. Doré, 142-159.

16. *Moe uchastie v Russkom Studencheskom Khristianskom Dvizhenii (My Participation in the Russian Student Christian Movement)*, 94, Vasilii Zen'kovskii, Box 1, Bakhmeteff Archive, Columbia University.

17. Michael K. Argus, *Moscow-on-the-Hudson* (New York, 1948), 153.

18. Commentary on Smith by Stella de Rosa Torgoff, "Immigrant Women, the Family, and Work: 1850-1950," Rosof et al., 44-45.

19. Tatiana Metternich, *Purgatory of Fools* (New York, 1976), 32.

20. Countess Marguerite Cassini, *Never a Dull Moment* (New York, 1956), 354.

21.Doré, 147-148.

22. Jean Anglade, *La vie quotidienne des immigrés en France de 1919 à jours* (Paris, 1976), 25.

23. Argus, 102.

24. Nina Berberova, *The Italics are Mine* (New York, 1969), 503.

25. Oldenbourg, 27.

26. "Altered Mood of Russian Refugees," *Interpreter*, 5, No. 4 (Apr. 1926): 9-10.

27. Richard Weiss, "Ethnicity and Reform: Minorities and the Ambience of the Depression Years," *J. of Amer. Hist.* 66, No. 3 (Dec. 1979), 585. Ronald H. Bayor, *Neighbors in Conflict — The Irish, Germans, Jews, and Italians of New York City, 1929-1941*, 2nd ed. (Urbana and Chicago, 1988), 164.

28. Argus, 108, 143.

29. Pierre Kovalevsky, *Zarubezhnaia Rossiia; istoriia i kul'turnoprosvetitel'naia rabota russkogo-zarubezh'ia za polveka (Emigré Russia; History and the Cultural-Educational Work of Russia Abroad for Half a Century, 1920-1970* (Paris, 1971), 36-37.

30. Sister Mary Edwarda, R.S.M., "The Russian Immigrant in the Lakewood Area of NJ: A Case Study," *International Migration Digest* 2 (Fall 1965): 142.

31. Paul Magocsi, "Russians," *Harvard Encyc. of Amer. Ethnic Groups* (Cambridge, MA, 1980), 891.

32. Zoé Oldenbourg, *La joie-souffrance* (Paris, 1980), 17.

94

INDEX